To Jane,
A new friend...

This Old World

Best, *[signature]*

Mike Lunsford

Author of *A Windy Hill Almanac* and
The Bridge That Carries You Over

—2021—

Shade Tree Press

Shade Tree Press
8945 South Coxville Rd.
Rosedale, Indiana 47874
www.mikelunsford.com

©Copyright 2020 by Mike Lunsford
All rights reserved

Printed in the United States of America

The author and publisher gratefully acknowledge the *Terre Haute Tribune-Star* in which the contents of this book appeared in column form.

Library of Congress Control Number: 2020903669

Cover art, *The Gathering Place*, courtesy of the artist, Lynne Dunnavant. Additional cover and title page art by Page Fetter. Author's photo by Joan Lunsford.

Lunsford, Michael J. (Mike), 1956-
This Old World/Mike Lunsford

ISBN (pbk.) 978-0-578-65412-6

To my family—those still with us and those gone—all who have shown me the way in this old world.

Foreword

Years ago, when my Grandfather Roy was still alive and I believed that he was not only a good man, but a great one, we were in the leafy mountains of Virginia, headed toward a little town on the Tennessee border where distant and annually-visited cousins lived. Whether it was for the first time or the fifth, I can't remember, but we stopped, as we did every year, along a two-lane highway where a busy stream poured over green rocks before it disappeared into the woods.

It was a spot where my grandmother—by then long asleep in our town's cemetery—used to ask him to stop so she could sit with her feet in the water for "a spell." The place was just a few miles from Gate City, where she was born. Long before I had ever been thought of, she had been my grandfather's traveling companion on thirty or more such trips.

We walked along the banks of the creek a while, listening to the comforting roar of the water bounce back to us from the stone walls of the ravine, and I breathed in, I think now, the cool air of his memories, for he would suddenly stop and stare a while at nothing in particular.

"This old world just keeps turning, whether we're here to feel it or not," he said, and with that thought hanging in the mist he headed back to his truck; our time there was over. For a while, it was a quiet drive eastward, but it didn't take long for him to shake off his melancholy, think of a joke, or point out the mist of a valley below us. "Look down in there," he'd say, pointing oddly with most of an open hand rather than with a single finger.

He was right, of course, in saying what he did, and I think that day comes back to me most, not in the solemn recollections of the days when I miss him, but when I am walking our own woods or sitting in the sun of a beach or wading the branch that wanders through my in-laws' old farm. The trees reach upward, the tides roll in, and the spring water runs over the time-worn gravel whether I am there to see or hear them get done. It is not a sad thing to think of at all, for in a world that seems to be changing so quickly and so much, it gives me a solid feeling to know that some things stay constant. That is unless we finally get around to clear-cutting or bulldozing everything in our way, which we often call "progress" and seem determined to do...

This collection of stories constitutes my seventh book. I know I have a few more in me, so this is no fare-thee-well; I still have plans. But, as I first began to string these tales together into a manuscript, I felt that most of those I kept back to use dealt with the permanence of things, or at least the things I want to last, my grandsons' childhoods, for instance; my own memories of childhood, another.

In his poem, "Our Real Work," Wendell Berry suggests that we may grow older, but don't necessarily get a whole lot figured out as we do it. "It may be that when we no longer know what to do," he writes, "we have come to our real work." I agree with that sentiment.

Over the past few years, I have retired from my chosen profession, but not from living my life. As these stories suggest, I spend much time walking my ground and breathing my air and asking questions. After all, "The mind that is not baffled is not employed," Berry adds in that poem.

There is one thing I do know: our planet, wrecked by our hands, or saved by them, will outlive us; this old world will keep turning. And I also know that I am thankful for those I have in my life, for my family and my friends. I think these stories suggest that too.

In the past few months, as this book came together, we have endured what may only be the beginning of a global pandemic and a new era of social unrest. I don't believe it will be the end of us, or is the end of the world. Our handhold may be precarious, but the planet will continue to spin.

So, here we go yet again; you can see if your money was well-spent. Thanks to my friends who encourage me and bother to read what I write, to my children and grandsons, who make me proud, and to my wife, Joanie, my partner in everything. And, thanks to my Grandfather Roy, who taught me a few things about this old world.

ML, May 2020

Table of Contents

The Blessings of a Winter Walk – 1
The Legendary Doc Wheat – 5
A Beach is Good for the Soul – 12
A Fine Summer for Bluebirds – 17
Books are the Weapons in the War of Ideas – 20
The Change 9/11 brought to America – 23
Off to Wisconsin and Now Home Again – 27
Consider the Buckeye – 30
The ABCs of PB&J – 34
The Voice of a Poet – 37
Hornets' Nest Staying Put for the Winter – 40
A Conservationist Before His Time – 43
Swan Song on a Winter's Day – 48
Proverbs, Idioms, and Grandpa-ese – 52
Cravings for Crayons Continues – 56
No Winter Lasts Forever – 60
Grandson's Curiosity a Good Thing – 64
How did it Get So Late So Soon? – 68
Stories From Our Fathers – 71
A Soft Maple and a Hard Place – 74
Raspberries in the Sun – 78
Celebrate Ernie Pyle for What He Was – 82

The Good of Simple Technology – 86
A Day at the Branch – 89
Something Magical About Sunflowers – 93
Brothers in Arms – 97
A Day Wasted Probably Wasn't – 101
Nothing New from the Western Front – 105
A Cardinal at my Window – 109
Thoughts of Silver Bells – 112
Rod Serling Speaks to Us – 116
Marion Jackson Was a Gift – 120
My Two Cents on Cents – 125
We Need to Truly Observe Earth Day – 129
The Morel of the Story – 133
'The Seasons Run With Swift Feet' – 137
The Old Man Who Planted a Tree – 140
The Pure Miracle of D-Day – 144
Checking One Off The Bucket List – 147
Summer Days With Creeks and Crawdads – 151
We Need Another American Moonshot – 155
The Music of the Stream – 159
The Shared Experience of Sunsets – 165
Wet Spring Brings Swallowtail Summer – 168
Spiderwebs Our 'Continents of Light' – 172
Because We Are Prone to Forget – 176
Nature's Custodial Engineers – 179
Jim and Clara's Boys – 183
The Making of Miner Brown – 188
The Flexible Flyer of Memory – 194
The Real Value of Field Trips – 198
Old Soldiers Never Die – 202

I wake to sleep, and take my waking slow.
I feel my fate in what I cannot fear.
I learn by going where I have to go.
Theodore Roethke

Attention is the beginning of devotion.
Mary Oliver

I tucked my trouser-ends in my boots
And went and had a good time.
Walt Whitman

It is only in the mind that shining adventure
remains forever bright.
Aldo Leopold

Mike Lunsford

This Old World

THE BLESSINGS OF A WINTER WALK
February 19, 2017

Despite owning a streak of wanderlust that usually gets a hold of me by early summer, I have never felt much desire to stay away for long from the place where I live. I am a hills and hollers man from way back, so the wooded valleys that reach out toward my southern Parke County home like arthritic fingers please me and give me the desire to stay put.

Living in such a place, however, doesn't mean I have no interest in still exploring it. So, over a month of Saturdays ago, and despite a stretch of the coldest weather of the winter, I knew before I ever threw off my bed covers that frosty morning that I wanted to take a walk—camera in hand—to a place across the Big Raccoon at the old Roseville Bridge.

Aldous Huxley—much in the news in these *Brave New World* days of ours—said that his father considered a good walk the equivalent of going to church. I may have been one day early and minus a preacher, but I had an expectation before I ever left the house of a glorious day,

This Old World

one that would constitute a blessing before it ended. I was not disappointed. After a few hours of padding about the kitchen—a trip to the bird feeder and paper box and barn thrown in—I swallowed a final gulp of black coffee and told my wife, as she read the newspaper over a late breakfast, that I was going for a walk. The sun by then was nearly as high in the sky as it could climb, but I could hear our front porch wind chimes banging out a terrible tune in the frigid breeze, so I knew any appearance of warmth on the other side of our windows was deceiving.

The look I got from her was expected; it was 5 degrees, and I considered for a moment the sight of our barn cat—usually at our back door on even the rawest mornings—as I had found him two hours before, still in his straw-fortified bed, wound as tight as a watch spring, nose tucked under his furry paws. His one open eye suggested that his tray needed to be left; that he'd be sleeping in for a while.

Thermal long johns, a stocking cap, L.L. Bean insulated boots, a scarf, and my best gloves constituted the most critical parts of my outfit. I loaded my camera bag with extra batteries, filled a water bottle and took off, having no plan other than to spend a few hours along Rock Run Creek, a winding little ribbon of water, most likely frozen after a week in the chest freezer of early January.

I was no stranger to the place I chose to wander that morning. Years ago, I waded in Rock Run Creek—at one time called Iron Run—with a grandmother who was certain there were no spots deep enough to concern us. More than once, with a brother or friend, we had been allowed access by the land's owner for an overnight camping trip. But it was all new to me again some 40 years later, and my day was the better for it.

Much to my surprise, the creek's water was running that day, waist deep in some places. Shelves of clifting ice reached out from the banks, but December's rains still ran in Rock Run's veins, crystal clear in some spots, roiled and sandy in others. Sycamores dot the creek's banks like untanned arms there, and huge exposures of sandstone jut from the surrounding hillsides, promontories left in place some 70,000 years ago during the last glacial age. Some of the rocks' carvings may be as fresh as 10,000 years, but since then erosion and wind and ice melt have formed the soil now tilled in surrounding fields.

My face and fingers grew numb within a few minutes of starting my hike, the creek to my right and steep tree-studded hills to my left. I eventually reached a point where I could walk no farther, unless I wanted to be wet to the knees, so I turned to hike along the creek back toward where it empties into its big brother, the Big Raccoon. I also climbed along a few of the sandstone ledges, and in doing so became an inspector of icicles and dried leaves, and an observer of blue skies and sycamore bark. In one place, I found in the snow the biggest turkey tracks I think I have ever seen. It seems that like me, he was a solitary rambler, out for a stroll with the same cold wind keeping him company.

With a branch serving as a seat, I sat and listened to the creek run a while, but with less blood pumping to my feet and hands, it didn't take long to grow uncomfortable and want to move on. In all, I spent three hours in the cathedral, the sky never wavering from the intense blue that became a rarity as the month grew older.

In 1871, E.T. Cox, the Indiana State Geologist, came to the area I wandered. He described it as a place that would hold "interest for both miner and geologist." He wrote that in some places the "carboniferous and conglomerate" sandstone abutments reached 40 feet in thickness, and that some of its more "beautiful white and friable stone" was making its way to Terre Haute for "glass making."

In that area, Cox says he found evidence that at one time the Big Raccoon ran southward, toward Vigo County, but "a wonderful disturbance of the rocks, for which our earth has been remarkable" turned it to run to the north and west where it began to empty into the Wabash (south of Montezuma) eons ago. He described the land above the area that I walked as "mellowing into soil-covered hills." It is on one of those hills that I live.

Not long after I got home that day, warm and in dry socks, a bowl of hot soup in my belly, I told Joanie of my adventures and how they had made me happy, like a boy. It was a blessing.

Mike Lunsford

THE LEGENDARY DOC WHEAT
July 16, 2017

If I had a quarter for every story I've heard about Doc Wheat burying his money, I'd be rich. But the fact is, some of the unlikely tales still told about the eccentric Parke County doctor are true ...

Born in 1870 in Roseville (now Coxville), Wallace W. Wheat—or "Doc," as he was called for nearly 50 years—seems to have been destined to practice medicine in the small town not far from where I live. A few of the sandstone foundation blocks from Doc's house—undoubtedly cut from the hillsides across Big Raccoon Creek—are tucked into one of my garden walls. I brought them home years ago, just before the old house was demolished.

The history of Parke County is rich with unconventional characters. The two most associated with Coxville—Hall-of-Fame pitcher Mordecai "Three-Finger" Brown and B-movie tough guy, Edward "Tex" Terry—put the town behind them for a while as they pursued their careers. But other than living in nearby Mecca for a short time, Wheat never really left, unless his three years at the Eclectic Medical Institute in Cincinnati (from 1896-1899) count. Of course, there are other stories of his trips away from Indiana: Wheat purportedly walked to medical conventions in distant cities, like St. Louis, acquiring medicinal plants along the way; legend has it that he did so in his bare feet.

This Old World

Those kinds of stories, still told at reunions and around campfires, keep Wheat's legacy alive, but as idiosyncratic as he might have been, he was, by all accounts, a very good doctor and an unconventional thinker. His popularity was such that on many occasions, Coxville Road—then called Yankee Street—was backed up a quarter of a mile in either direction with Model T's. His patients simply got in line and paid "a dollar-and-a-dime" to see a man who practiced using the medicines he made himself.

One of Doc's patients was Estel Fisher. Now 81 and living in Florida, Fisher grew up just across the creek, near Tick Ridge; he graduated from Rosedale High School in 1954.

"I got to know Doc a little when he came across the creek to get water from our spring-fed well. A lot of the water around Coxville was tainted with iron from the coal mines, and he wanted good water to make his medicines with. I know that he eventually had cisterns to collect it," Fisher told me.

Jeff and Stephanie Hasler now own part of Doc's property, and hope to eventually build on the ridge above the road. A few muggy nights ago, I explored a bit with Jeff, a trek that took us mostly straight up. He showed me both of the cisterns Doc built; the first at nearly the top of the slope is, by Jeff's estimation, large enough to hold about 17,000 gallons of water. It was an amazing feat to get the materials—particularly the concrete—up that hill. A stamped inscription on the cistern lid reads, "WW Wheat,

Nov. 6, 1928." A smaller cistern at the bottom of the hill was originally located inside Doc's stable, and remnants of piping suggest it was gravity-filled from the tank above.

Besides a good water source for making tinctures, Wheat hated the inconsistencies of living without electrical power. He used the cisterns to supply water for the boilers that heated the house (primarily inhabited by his nephew, Elbert, and his family) across the road, but also used them to generate his own electrical power until the REMC came to Coxville. Because of his ingenuity, Wheat was able to grow exotic plants—even oranges—in his heated greenhouse.

"I'm just fascinated with the stories about this man," Hasler said, as he wiped sweat from his forehead. And, just to make the record clear, he's never found a dime anywhere near the property.

Wheat was an "eclectic" physician, a firm believer in botanical medicines. Eclectics were very popular in the Midwest well past the turn into the 20th century; they believed that the body was capable of healing itself if helped with natural curatives.

According to Laura Clavio, author of *The Eclectic: The Life and Times of Wallace Wheat*, the Eclectic Institute was a leading school of medicine in the late 1800s, reaching its peak about the time Doc attended college. "The Lloyd Library of Cincinnati holds the records of the Eclectic movement and has one of the largest botanical libraries in the world that is used by scientists from all over the world today," she says.

"I think Doc may have been eccentric to some, but a lot of it was legend," Clavio added. "He was mostly a very intelligent man who solved his own problems, lived simply, and lived to help others. People don't realize that the Eclectics were the forerunners of today's naturopaths. They made a huge contribution that has gone largely unrecognized."

Fisher agrees; he said he went to Wheat, "... mostly for sore throats and coughs," and Doc, who was by that time in his 70s, "had a hallway that was lined with big glass jugs filled with medicine." He added: "I always came away from his office with a small bag of figs too, because Doc believed it was important to stay regular. So he handed out those figs and reminded people to eat them."

Fisher also recalled the day when he and a couple of his buddies were playing along the railroad tracks, and they ventured into the open basement door of Doc's house. "We saw a skeleton, and decided to not go the rest of the way in," he said, then added that the skeleton was real. Doc had acquired a body to study muscle tissue and bone structure, and had knitted the bones together himself after dissection.

"I believe he really knew what he was doing; he wasn't a quack," Estel says. He made house calls, but most people saw him in his office, "and people came from all over—even Illinois. Sally Gregg used to set up a lemonade stand along the road and sell it to Doc's customers on hot days."

Besides the greenhouse he built onto the south side of the house, Wheat also had an apple and peach orchard across the road and a large garden. He built an expansive concrete cellar too, using it not only for making medicine, but as a summer hospital, a cool place to meet with patients in the heat of summer; one room was used for hydrotherapy sessions. The cellar was recently recalled by Doc's namesake, great-great-nephew Wallace Wayne Wheat, who grew up in Rosedale, but now lives in Louisville.

"I remember that as a young teenager, I explored his abandoned home site and the cave [cellar] looking for treasure. Of course, there was none to be found. Its entrance and underground structure was framed with formed cement and was very dark, musty, and damp inside. Toward the front of the cave were the remains of an American flag painted on one of the walls," Wayne said.

Doc's original office wasn't in his home, although he did attach one on the east side of the big house sometime during the Great Depression. Various members of the Wheat clan regularly helped by organizing patients, working in the yard, and feeding livestock. Before he moved into the new office — perhaps soon after Elbert's death in 1931 — Wheat's office sat just a few feet from the Chicago and Eastern Illinois railroad tracks that ran through town. Once a two-story house that had been reduced to just its top floor, it was situated near a corner that still leads passers-by across the covered bridge. Wheat mostly lived there; peculiarly, sleeping on the floor.

In 1910, Wheat photographed the nearby bridge (built by J.J. Daniels) as it burned and fell into the creek. He went on to capture images of the crews that built the new bridge and also took pictures of the children who had to use a rope bridge to get across the creek to the schoolhouse. The two arsonists convicted of burning the bridge went to prison, but a more compelling story was to come to Coxville 15 years later.

There is little doubt that the tales about Wheat's distrust of banks are true, for like many others, even before the hard years of the '30s, he had lost money when local institutions crashed. His legend has been magnified by the lore of the thousands of dollars that were supposedly discovered buried on his property after his death, much of it said to be found in canning jars. The habit nearly cost him his life.

One night in the summer of 1925, three men from Lafayette who had somehow heard of the doctor without a bank, and in hopes of an easy score, broke into the office, held carbide lamps to Wheat's feet—even doused him with kerosene and threatened to light him on fire—in an attempt to persuade him to reveal where he had hidden his money. Doc's brother, Albert, was tied up and forced to watch the terrible scene in which holes were burned completely through Wheat's feet. Yet the criminals fled the office with nothing after a crossing bell at the nearby train tracks began to ring; inexplicably, no train was coming down the tracks ... Wheat spent several miserable months in a wheelchair, yet chose to treat himself with the help of a fellow eclectic physician. He suffered from foot problems the rest of his life.

Stories about Wheat may be fading as those who can accurately recall him leave us. For instance, Glenn Fisher, who died just a few years ago, used to stop by when he'd see me mowing my yard, and more than once Doc became a shade tree conversation. Glenn, a very distant cousin of Estel, often hunted ginseng and worked at odd jobs for Wheat, including some with a local teen named Sam who played a role in yet another crime against the physician.

In early 1947, the boy discovered some money while working in Wheat's barn; he later drove to Kentucky and bragged about his easy windfall. Four of Sam's acquaintances there hatched a plan to steal from Wheat while he was away from the house, and had it not been for the observant Rosedale town marshal getting suspicious, the robbery, which netted over $4,000, would have succeeded. Instead, the men were captured after a shoot-out with authorities in northern Vigo County, and Sam was eventually implicated as being complicit.

The subsequent trial was a local sensation, and hundreds from the community attended, including classes from Rosedale High School. According to Clavio, agents of the Internal Revenue Service came too, for it is doubtful that Wheat was in the habit of reporting all of his income.

Doc Wheat never married; he was once engaged, but why that relationship ended is yet another story. He owned a car, but hired someone else to drive him, and it is a strong possibility that he may have used his own personal battle with cancer as a way to study possible cures... How much of his money was found was never known—although some most certainly was—but there was hardly a spot in his yard and orchard that wasn't pockmarked with shoveled holes or covered with metal detectors years ago.

Clavio believes—as do others—that Wheat was working on important medical research; some claimed he was close to discovering a cure for cancer, but those secrets went with him to the grave.

Wheat loved his neighbors and community, and often invited most of the town's residents to come by for a celebration supper or Thanksgiving dinner; the last of those came in November 1947, less than a year before he died.

Dr. Wallace Wheat is buried in Rosedale Cemetery, and unlike his money, it is there he remains ...

A BEACH IS GOOD FOR THE SOUL
July 17, 2017

I have written many times over the years about our annual pilgrimage to the Lake Michigan shoreline, yet, here I am again, trying to relate to my friends just how much the blue-green water and its waves mean to us.

This year, we headed a little farther north to a rented house in South Haven, for the wonderful Great Depression-era cabins that we have stayed in for years also require rigorous trips up and down a steep set of stairs to and from the beach. Despite being senior citizens now, Joanie and I can still hack the climb, but we thought it best not to put our pregnant daughter-in-law through such daily workouts, lest we have our second grandchild earlier than expected.

In a series of features about yet a more extensive tour of Michigan last summer—we left the rest of the family at home for that one—I extolled the virtues of the many towns we visited, but had little to say about South Haven, which boasts a wonderful downtown, tastefully-designed homes, and a splendid old red lighthouse. It is a beautiful little town, but after the day we spent there, we came away feeling rushed, as if we had been through a typical tourist trap wringer and left hanging out to dry.

I take all of that back now, for we loved the place this summer, and I have learned, once again, that first impressions are often wrong.

Despite a few early days of very cool weather that kept everyone out of the water, and a stiff breeze that tossed our hair about like salads, we enjoyed good food, a nice daily walk or bike ride to the beach, and a quiet little sandy promontory above the water where we could hide in the tall grass, pretty much away from everyone else.

My grandson and son eventually made it into the chilly lake, but not without a little teeth chattering and shivering. I, on the other hand, did as I always do: watched the water and read books and dozed in a beach chair, and then I did it all over again. That is my idea of a real vacation, with a few crosswords thrown in for good measure.

Red warning flags blew stiffly in a rather raw wind as we first arrived at South Haven. Typical road construction along I-94, that seems to be in place like a plague of locusts in time for our annual trip, had slowed us in getting there. So after unpacking, the late hour left us little time to do much more than eat supper, bundle up a bit, and head to the lake to watch the sun set. We are rarely disappointed in a Lake Michigan sunset, and despite hugging ourselves to stay warm, we witnessed a blue-ribbon winner that first night.

Joanie and I spent most of the rest of our days on the beach, her hair uncharacteristically stuffed under one of my ball caps, and both of us toting books under one arm and chairs under the other. We soon discovered that several bikes—we chose retro Schwinns—were available for our use, and I eventually became a pro at strapping everything we needed to the back of mine. It did take a few minutes to adjust to the bike's coaster brake, for I don't think I've used one since I was 12.

Over the course of the week I filled the spaces around my crosswords with lists of observations that really described—in scribbles—our stay at South Haven. For instance, we noticed that there were virtually no stones on these beaches, so our traditional rock-skipping competition had to be called off. We also noticed a number of ducks flying overhead; we never see those where we normally stay, and one eventually posed rather nicely for my camera one morning. Within an hour of snapping the mallard's picture, I took another of a "Jolly Roger" flying over a pleasure boat quite far out on the lake, but we never felt a pillaging raid was imminent.

As usual, I noted how the different angle of the sun—from the morning through the supper hours—changed the color of the lake all day. In fact, color is what I most notice on these trips. Milkweed was growing everywhere along the beach, and I saw monarch butterflies flitting about it, and black squirrels in the yards, and brown house wrens everywhere.

Of course, the gulls (both ring-billed and herring) are always present along the beach. Most are looking for handouts of cookies and crackers, but they dominated the view nearly as much as the incoming surf, often flying startlingly close to us. The birds I was most interested in, however, were the bank swallows that occupied the steep sandy cliff that we sat atop. I often walked down to the beach to try to catch them in a photo as they entered and exited the caverns they'd excavated in the banks, but was never able to do it. They were so fast, so nearly manic, that I could never get them in my viewfinder, so I eventually quit trying.

By our second or third day, the red flags had been replaced with yellow, and the temperatures lifted well into the 70's. Joanie and I biked down to the pier to walk out to

This Old World

the lighthouse—built in 1903 of cast iron and painted bright red—and to watch a few fisherman casting for steelhead. The beach near there was quite crowded, so we soon retreated and headed back to base for lunch.

It may sound odd, but my favorite day on the lake was one which promised rain. On one late afternoon, we could see storm clouds gathering to the west—even saw a waterspout off in the distance—and the sun played a game of tag with the lake, turning it alternating shades of blue, then green and brown as the waves stirred up sand along the beach. The marram grass bent in the strong breeze, and slowly, but surely, the beaches emptied as people grew tired of chasing umbrellas and hats, and the supper hour approached.

I stayed on to watch the show, and was glad I did. The choppy whitecaps and green water and purple-blue rain clouds came in across the distant pier, and just then I knew that I hadn't seen many places in my life that were much prettier.

On the mantle of the house we had rented, the owner had placed one of those typical beach-related curios, sometimes picked up at yard sales when the original buyer has grown tired of northern climes and has headed to Arizona. It was, if I recall now, a bit of driftwood glued to a small sign that read, "A beach is good for the soul."

Yes, it sure is.

Mike Lunsford

A FINE SUMMER FOR BLUEBIRDS
July 31, 2017

This has been a good summer around my place for bluebirds. In past years, I have seen only a few fidgeting about our yard and along the woods. They are pleasant dashes of color and bits of song among those of our usual house wrens and cardinals and sparrows. But this year has brought them to us in concert, and I hope they have found a home.

Earlier this spring I spent about every free hour I had wandering my woods and slogging along the creek, camera in hand. For some reason, I took an inordinate number of bluebird photographs, mostly in a place not far from us where rotting tree trunks are dotted by woodpecker holes like machine gun bullet-riddled targets. The woodpeckers—particularly the big and bossy red-headed variety—still rule the roost there, but the bluebirds seemed to have moved in just after the snows left, and it appears court orders will be needed to get them out.

Because I have watched—and heard—so many bluebirds (they are actually a type of thrush), I decided early to set up a few more nesting boxes about my yard this spring. Several aren't in ideal spots, and I knew the little brown house wrens that chatter all day long and make raids on our cat's food dishes, were determined to claim them all. But just a few days ago, I saw a bluebird pop out of a nesting box I have nailed under the eaves to the back of my storage barn, so they now seem to have planted a blue,

This Old World

white, and orange flag in the yard, where before wren brown and nuthatch gray dominated the scene.

I believe I have cleaned bluebird nests out of a few of my boxes in past autumns and never knew it, but now I am reading a bit about them and know that they like to weave a bowl of fine long grasses and pine needles—deep enough to drop about four eggs into. Bluebirds apparently don't mind snoops like me peering into or checking on their nests for they are often raided by other birds, and apparently appreciate a little human presence.

By the way, I have also cleared house wren nests away in the fall, and I just learned that they will often build false nests—just a jumble of twigs—to discourage other birds from using empty boxes. Wrens are very pretty little birds, rotund with intricate feathering, but they were so noisy a week or so ago as I stained my cabin siding that I wished they had a mute button. They were irritated that I was near one of their boxes, the ingrates, for I am the one who put it in place. And now, I know that they are also neighborhood snobs.

Indiana State University professor emeritus Peter Scott—who I frequently pester with questions about birds—tells me that although bluebird habitats are being threatened by encroaching land development, they aren't doing too badly in our area.

"Bluebirds hold their own very well around here. Rural Indiana, at least our area, seems good for them. Whenever I am biking in summer, or birding by car in winter, I see them regularly on the roadside wires. They are permanent residents—not much sign of migration—and they are remarkably hardy. The ability to feed on fruit probably helps in winter," Scott says.

"The woodland patches provide shelter in winter, and that means they can start early to breed. Some pairs at least have time for two broods. As cavity nesters, they have to compete with certain other species that depend on woodpecker holes and nest boxes. Competitors include house wrens, tree swallows, house sparrows, chickadees, and titmice," he added, while making sure that he also told me he was no "expert on bluebirds."

Unlike other species of birds, there isn't a lot of difference between male and female bluebirds (we are talking about Eastern bluebirds here—*sialia sialis*); the female's colors are usually a bit more muted, so they appear as being more gray or brown. As is the case with cardinals though, I often find the female bluebirds prettier than their flashier mates.

The bluebirds that I have seen around always seem to be perched on an old lopsided privacy fence, never far from the security of the woods, and like robins—which I wrote about a few months ago—they aren't attracted to feeders, unless offered insects (my *Sibley Guide to Birds* suggests mealworms). They tend to sit on roadside wires and fence posts, dropping to the ground to grab a bug or berry, and they make quite a show about it too. So, most often, the best we can do is provide a place for them to nest and let them take care of their own diets.

I should be happy that bluebirds have been slowly, but surely, coming our way. By August, as many of our garden flowers fade and the roadside weeds go to seed and take on scraggly and worn-out faces, we need the colors that birds and butterflies provide.

Now, all I have to do is convince our wrens to leave their neighbors alone.

BOOKS ARE WEAPONS IN THE WAR OF IDEAS
August 28, 2017

I opened our newspaper this morning and saw a photo of Ray Parks. Ray was shown riding in an open jeep, tossing candy out to folks at a parade during Dana's Ernie Pyle Festival. He served in World War II, and is one of a handful of veterans I have been privileged to know.

Seeing Ray, and what he represents, makes me realize that our country—despite the ugliness of Charlottesville, the political chaos in Washington, and the threats of the North Koreans—will be alright, that is if we in the generations that follow his are decent neighbors and good friends and responsible citizens.

I have written before about my old friends—people like Bill Engle, who fought at the Battle of the Bulge in the cold of 1944; I spoke with him just last Sunday morning. I also recall conversations I had with three of my great uncles; they went to that war and were in it when they learned that another brother had been killed not far from the

German border. I wish everyone I know—the very last classes of students I'll teach, included—could meet men like them, and listen to their stories and witness their humor and plainspoken honesty and humility. It would be interesting to hear what these men have to say, or would have said, about those who held Nazi flags at the University of Virginia a few weeks ago.

The photo of Ray also conjured thoughts of Ernie Pyle, too. If you have never read anything by him, you should; he is among the very best writers this country has produced. I have read his *Brave Men* and *Last Chapter*, and I recall one of his frontline columns about seeing German prisoners hemmed behind barbed wire. He wasn't too impressed with them, other than to say that they didn't look like "supermen" to him. They looked defeated, and vain, and very human. He described how some mugged for a reporter's camera; others took off their shirts and sat in the sun. All of them knew the war was coming to an end, and that they had lost it.

By coincidence, I have just finished my reading of Molly Guptill Manning's wonderful *The Books That Went to War*. Her stories describe the programs that produced the "American Service Editions," the millions of books, of all kinds and titles that went to Europe and Africa and the Pacific with our servicemen and women in World War II. Time and time again, Manning provides letters from grateful soldiers and airmen and sailors, who not only faced the Germans and Japanese in combat but also the endless

This Old World

boredom and anxieties of war.

"Oh, I sure remember those books," Bill told me. "They were practically our Bibles. We loved them."

The average readers of ASE's didn't have high school diplomas, yet they craved the specially-designed classics and best-sellers sent their way. I won't soon forget the image put into my head as Manning mentioned a letter from a soldier who wrote about a detail in which he prepared a GI for burial; there was a copy of *Their Hearts Were Young and Gay* still tucked in the dead man's back pocket.

The ASE books were the result of a program called the "Council on Books in Wartime," and its slogan was, "Books are Weapons in the War of Ideas." Franklin Roosevelt, who provided the eloquence all real leaders supply when it is needed, said of the Nazi's obsession with burning books: "Books can not be killed by fire. People die, but books never die. No man and no force can abolish memory... In this war, we know, books are weapons. And it is a part of your dedication always to make them weapons for man's freedom."

I've thought quite a lot about the anger of those who marched under swastikas at Charlottesville, their arms raised in Hitleresque salutes in the same places where Thomas Jefferson—not perfect, but brilliant and idealistic—designed the enlightened curriculum that reflected the American people's thirst for education and great books and the miracles of inquisitiveness and knowledge. It has made me wonder why books like those that bolstered and taught the troops that fought for democracy in World War II are playing less and less of a role in the educations of our children today.

It was a terrible thing to watch Americans chant in that torch-lit Nuremberg-like rally, and I know there is hope by many across the country that displays like it will just go away. But that march did reinforce one thing: Freedom and democracy have always been best served by people who read books, not burn them.

THE CHANGE 9/11 BROUGHT TO AMERICA
September 11, 2017

Like most Americans who are old enough, I can remember exactly where I was on the morning of September 11, 2001, as the news broke of the murderous terrorist assault on America.

I was at my schoolroom desk; the day had just begun—a first period prep hour—and I was grading senior essays, a cup of coffee occasionally exchanging places with a red ballpoint pen. One of my best students, Jenna Stevens, ran through the doorway, breathless, begging me to turn on my television, that a passenger jet had hit the World Trade Center in New York.

Those were the pre-wireless days; not many of us even had cell phones yet, particularly students, so I did as I was asked, fiddled a bit with the television's old rabbit ears, and hoped for the best reception. It was nearly 9 a.m.

This Old World

Of course, very few people knew so early that we were actually under attack, that is until the second plane—United Airlines Flight 175—hit the south tower.

Within minutes, President Bush, grim-faced and stoic, was told as he sat in a Florida elementary school classroom, and Flight 77 hit the Pentagon.

The collapse of both towers, the horrible sights carried live of innocents jumping from fiery windows to their deaths, the heroics of the passengers on Flight 93 and the first responders, were still unfolding stories. But by then my room had filled with students—only some of which were actually in my second period class—and they sat in total silence, watching the snowy pictures. Some cried.

Things have not quite been the same in this country since that day; in the world, now that I think of it. It was like other jumping off points in American history, like the January day the Space Shuttle Challenger exploded; I was watching over a study hall in the library at Montezuma, and we all learned of it on the radio. I was in second grade the day John Kennedy was killed—a late November day that played out with a tiny television and a rabbit-eared antenna too.

A few of my older friends tell me they sensed the same feelings when they heard that Franklin Roosevelt had died, or that the Japanese had attacked Pearl Harbor; that somehow, in some way, the world was going to be different from that day forward.

"I was still getting my undergraduate degree at

Kentucky Christian University, and that Tuesday was Chapel day," said Adam Coffman, a 38-year-old minister. "Chapel began at 10 in the morning, and I had no classes before that, so I had just gotten out of bed and dressed, and was still half asleep when I entered the chapel and sat down," he said.

"I hadn't talked to anyone yet, so the first I heard about what was happening was when the campus minister took to the stage, asked for everyone's attention, then told that we were under attack. He went on to give us the details he knew, then prayed and dismissed us early. The other classes I had were canceled that day, and I mainly just remember watching the news, and calling my parents who were back home in Indiana."

Coffman believes the country changed that day: "I think it was the initial spark that ignited a fire of anger and fear, a fire that has since burned its way through every nook and cranny of our society. And it's a fire that seems to only be growing. There are so many things that have contributed to it. I don't want to oversimplify, but I feel like 9/11 was the beginning of that," he said.

"Our country was infected with the diseases of fear, anger, hate, and aggression on 9/11, and 16 years later we've become so full of it that we're tearing ourselves apart in response," he says. "We all know it's not who we really are deep down, not what our country is supposed to be, but it's what we've become. There's still hope, but it takes extraordinary acts of kindness and compassion for our fellow man—regardless of who they are, where they are from, their politics or their religion—in order to make any kind of progress in dousing the fire that's consuming us and healing the cancer that's making us sick," he added.

Shirley Brown is a half-century older than Coffman; she's lived in a small town (Rosedale) her entire life, and she sees the events of 9/11 through a longer lens of history. "I have lived through a lot of special times, and I am still living them in my memories," she said.

"I was using the sweeper with the television on when I heard about Kennedy's assassination, and I was working in the Town Hall [as the treasurer] when the space shuttle exploded. I listened about it on the radio, and on my lunch hour I went up to Virginia Pastorius's house so I could see it on TV."

"But when 9/11 happened, I was taking my daily walk and came in as Everett [Shirley's husband of 68 years who passed a year ago last spring at 89] said, 'Watch the television; a plane has hit the tower in New York.' Well, we watched the rest of the day, and the day after, and the day after that, and I'll never forget it. We were on vacation a year later, and we watched an anniversary program, and I was very upset to see it happen all over again; I think of it every year."

"I'm sorry to say it," Shirley adds, "but I am unhappy with the way this country has gone since then. I was taught to respect the people that serve our country, and also to maintain the history of it. My husband was a veteran of World War II and the Korean War; my brother also served. I was taught to honor our flag and also our national anthem, and I get very upset when that doesn't happen. After 9/11, things changed, and I don't know why."

I think my friends are right; we have changed. But Americans have proven time and time again that we can rise to the occasion when we need to. As hurricanes batter us, North Korea threatens us, and the specter of terrorism always haunts us, it's time we do it again.

OFF TO WISCONSIN, AND NOW HOME AGAIN
September 25, 2017

We have just returned from another one of our wandering vacation trips, this time to the wet woods of Wisconsin. Of course, we're glad to be home, but that doesn't mean we were happy to leave, despite the fact that I regularly donated blood to the clouds of local mosquitoes there.

As anyone who reads my stories knows, Joanie and I—as persnickety as we usually are—vacation by the seat of our pants. We decide in what direction we want to head, agree on at least one place we wish to stop, and hope that everything turns out for the good. We have yet to be disappointed, although we do usually have to spend at least one night in a hotel straight out of a horror novel, and this year was no exception.

For a good while we weren't sure whether we were headed to Wisconsin to visit Frank Lloyd Wright or to West

This Old World

Virginia to ride a steam locomotive through the mountains, but since it was so hot and muggy here on the eve of our departure we decided that driving north might be the better of the two options. For the most part, the heat followed us anyway.

In case you might be thinking that we were sorely discouraged to discover upon knocking on his door that Wright has been dead for almost 60 years, we weren't; we were aware of his mortality but just wanted to see his house, "Taliesin," which sits near the little town of Spring Green and is open for walking tours. I have taught a bit about his architecture in one of my classes for years, even toured one of his "Prairie Houses," but I wanted to see his home, which grows out of the fertile hillsides near the banks of the Wisconsin River like the sumac and hollyhocks he so greatly admired.

We hold no animosity to those who feel their vacations are best spent among hordes of tourists, but we both have eclectic streaks, meaning we must roam a bit.

This trip led us to mostly quiet places: a short hike to a wonderful little waterfall; the great architect's house and its incredible story; a remote cabin among the pines planted by conservationist Aldo Leopold; the upstairs study of Pulitzer Prize winning novelist Hamlin Garland; the slender pavement of U.S. Highway 35 that meanders along the Mississippi River; a tiny town that boasts an amazing grotto; and two more memorable spots as we drove home through the endless cornfields of Illinois.

Mike Lunsford

In all, we traveled only about 1,200 miles, most coming on little state highways that halve hundreds of tiny towns and burgs dating back to the days of the Blackhawk War, and before. It is a region known as the "Driftless" area, for unlike so much of the rest of Wisconsin, it wasn't touched much by the last great glacial epoch that scoured out the Great Lakes and bulldozed most of Illinois and Indiana into pool table-flat farmland.

Of course, this journey leads me—and you—to a short series of monthly feature stories. There won't be many—perhaps four or so—as I already had plans to write of other things before the snow blows, but since I took my camera along and snapped too many pictures to count, I feel I have to share not only what we learned, but, of course, much of what we saw.

There were surprises, like the beauty of the mist that rose from the cool water beneath Stephens Falls as it was caught for just minutes in the morning sunlight; the huge pelicans we saw feeding in the Rock River near Dixon, Illinois; the small, but apparently prosperous, book store that feeds the intellectually curious in Spring Green; the female red-winged blackbird that repeatedly posed for me atop a spike of mullein near De Soto; the pair of beautiful 1928 Buick touring cars we saw in the parking lot near Taliesin; the massive steel arches being hoisted into place on a new bridge across the muddy Mississippi River…

We love to travel and see and learn, but we are always glad to be home too. As we ate supper one evening in La Crosse, the great river to our backs, we learned of the storms that hit near home, and despite assurances from those who watch over our place that we had virtually nothing damaged, I feared that when I pulled into our drive, I'd find a mess waiting for me.

The scene reminded me of a poem by Jane Kenyon called, "Coming Home at Twilight in Late Summer." Like us, she and her husband had been on a trip, and she wrote of, "… the unpacking, the mail and papers/the grass needed mowing…." But in the end, she wrote about how "grateful" they were to be home.

What we saw this year—what we have seen over all the years—has been wonderful. But we were grateful to be home too.

CONSIDER THE BUCKEYE
October 10, 2017

The dry weather this fall has already brought many of our leaves to their brown and rattling knees, and those who make a living at forecasting the weather are telling us that this season will be one without much color to it. A tall hackberry tree I have in my yard bears crunchy witness to that, despite finding an inch of rain in my gauge last week.

But consider for a moment the buckeye; it is among the first of the local trees to shed, even in good years for color and rain. Already pitted and pocked and yellowed, buckeye leaves are caught up in mowing or breezes long before we are looking for our yard rakes. Most of the trees, whether shaded or not, are bare long before now. But, it isn't their hand-shaped leaflets that are treasured anyway; it's their fruit.

I admire buckeyes so much that I have a century-old Mason jar filled with the seeds. I have picked them up over the years, and the jar sits on a bookcase in what used to be my office.

I look at them every once in a while, for they are curious bits of the natural world that clearly can't be improved upon, like blue jay feathers and pine cones and water-sanded driftwood; I have picked those up to bring home, too.

Buckeyes are considered by some to be talismans; old-timers used to advise that a buckeye in your pocket was a way to keep the rheumatism and gout away; others just claimed they were good luck.

I've never put faith in them or four-leaf clovers or rabbits' feet, but who am I to say that those who do are wrong?

I spotted a hornet's nest in my woods last week, not 10 feet off the ground; I believe I already have three of those. According to some folklorists, a nest that low suggests a mild winter is on its way, and that is something I wholeheartedly hope proves true. I don't place my trust in hornets or persimmon seeds or woolly bear caterpillars either, but there are those who do, and they are right as often as they are wrong.

Buckeyes are deceptively beautiful trees. Their

wood is light and fairly soft, and hasn't much use, although artificial limbs and spoons were once made of it. In the early spring, their beautiful red-orange buds are prominent long before most other leaves appear, and, as friend Marion Jackson writes in his *101 Trees of Indiana*, their bark is "ash-gray; smooth when young...fissured on older trees."

The trees I know best are Ohio Buckeyes (*Aesculus glabra*), and most are growing inconveniently along a wetlands, which means about half of their spiny nut hulls—which form in clumps near the ends of branches—drop into scummy water, their beauty ending up in no one's pocket at all.

The seeds—a wonderful chestnut brown with an obvious tan spot, like a deer's eye—are toxic and supposedly inedible, although it is obvious that the squirrels—perhaps a groundhog or two—eat them. Each year I race into the fall woods to grab them before they are all swallowed on the spot.

The buckeye's hulls most often split on contact with the ground, and the squirrels seem to be waiting for them to drop. This fall, I actually stood under one tree and tossed a small branch repeatedly up into the hulls, bringing a rain of them onto the grass below. I pried them open like treasure chests, finding nearly always two, but often three buckeyes in each.

Ohio buckeye trees are also called "fetid" or "stinking" buckeye, but since I don't pry the bark from trunks or snap limbs, I can't say I have ever noticed their smell. The hulls, even when a bit moist, don't stink at all, and they dry and wither to half their size in a day of tanning in the sun. It is hard to even find buckeyes this late into the season.

A few weeks ago, I had a class of my seniors—what will be my last group—read Scott Russell Sanders' wonderful essay, "Buckeye," which is mostly about his father and a trip back to his native Ohio ground, by then covered by a man-made lake.

Several of my students had no idea what a buckeye was; they had never seen or held one, which I remedied by bringing in a bag of fresh seeds, telling them to take a few for themselves. I am a little happier knowing that they'll now know what a buckeye is; who knows what they may find by doing a little snooping in the woods themselves.

My boyhood home ground had no buckeye trees. We had red oak and persimmon and beech in abundance, even a few shagbark hickories that dropped nuts that I hulled and ate, but I had to walk a mile or more to the west to find buckeyes. My brother and I used to camp near Spring Creek, often in very late fall, and across the stream from where we pitched our tent and built a fire, I found a grove of buckeyes and paw paws. It has been at least 45 years since I last walked under those trees, and I had forgotten about that special place until I began to write this piece, so, in a way, maybe buckeyes are good luck.

I told a friend last week that I was writing a story about buckeyes, and she immediately remembered a big

tree that stood on the corner of Main and Miller Streets, near Dee Cottrell's funeral home in Rosedale, years ago. "I always went home with one in my pocket," she said.
I understand why.

THE ABC'S OF PB&J
October 16, 2017

My grandson came down with a touch of something last week, so my wife got a late-night call that she'd be needed to look after him on a day that normally includes her errand running and grocery shopping. "You're going to have to settle for a peanut butter and jelly sandwich for lunch tomorrow," she told me as if the news was a bad report from the doctor.

For some reason, she, and a good many others, must feel that PBJ is a step down from the usual chicken salad or sliced ham or roast beef I normally take to work. But I don't think that way at all; the change in menu actually made me pretty happy.

I have always figured that a guy like me—one who doesn't fix his own lunches—has no right to complain about anything he finds in his lunchbox. It is an old story, but a family favorite that I may very well have mentioned before, that my Grandfather Roy once complained to my grandma that he was tired of the lunches she fixed for his factory "dinner pail." It seemed she had gotten into a bit of a lunch-fixing rut, and since he hadn't said anything before, she presumed he liked what she prepared for him.

Mike Lunsford

"Couldn't you, just once, use some imagination?" he complained to her surprise, one evening. The next day at noon he found two walnuts and a small tack hammer in his lunch box. Needless to say, he never whined on the subject again.

I love peanut butter and jelly sandwiches, and have since I took them to school in a yellow metal school bus-shaped lunchbox in my grade school days. Opening that lid in the cafeteria—it had two matching buckles—was heavenly, for the scents emanating from it not only smelled of freedom—no math book; no cursive practice—but also an end to my rumbling belly, at least until I could eat an after-school bowl of cereal at home.

With two cartons of cold white milk on the side, a PBJ sandwich is one of the finest and simplest pleasures life offers. Propping one's cold feet next to a hickory wood fire, not having to set an alarm clock, and standing under a hot shower are all fine things, indeed, but biting into the middle of a peanut butter and jelly sandwich is a most satisfying experience.

I got to pondering PBJs after friend Bart Colwell sent a-let's-just-chat email last month. For some reason, peanut butter and jelly came up in the conversation, and I apparently made a culinary faux pas by mentioning that I was happy to smear apple, raspberry, grape, or even that most enigmatically-labeled, "mixed fruit" jelly on my sandwiches.

Bart is a most accommodating guy, but he found my

This Old World

use of just any kind of jelly, well, Philistine. There are apparently some dignifying proprieties when it comes to PBJ.

"Okay, I may have to take issue with you on something," he wrote. "A true PBJ sandwich consists of the following: only white bread (and not the 35 calorie stuff that tastes like cardboard), a bunch of butter, a bunch of peanut butter, and 'Welch's Grape Jelly' [though 'Smucker's' will do in a pinch]."

This is a man who obviously knows his pectin. "You'll have to sell me on the blackberry jelly, which is great on toast, but I'm not sure about PBJ," he added. Now, some may call my friend a "PBJ snob," although I prefer, "purist." Bart is someone who takes his PBJ seriously, as do I, but mostly when it comes to its proper preparation. I have always felt that to get the best flavor, one needs to have an aged sandwich, not unlike the best wines, although I actually mean overnight (at least for a few hours in a grade school coat closet, and preferably in a brown paper sack). That way, the jelly has had proper time to soak a bit into the bread; it enhances the flavor, I think.

Let it also be known that I will eat peanut butter and jelly on whole wheat bread, not just white, but, of course, never on rye. I can go with or without the butter, and I can live with crunchy or smooth peanut butter.

One of my favorite recurring, yet minor, television characters is "Leon," the little cowboy-hat wearing kid (played by Clint Howard, brother of Ronny) who wanders

Mayberry's streets in *The Andy Griffith Show* and silently offers his peanut butter sandwich (only once do I recall his having jelly) to Andy or Barney, even Mr. Meldrim, the bank president. "No thanks, Leon," was their usual response.

Boy, they didn't know what they were missing.

THE VOICE OF A POET
November 20, 2017

There have been dozens of writers over the years that have inspired me to habitually put words on paper. For those critics out there who wish I had never learned how—or don't think I'm very good at it—I should supply a list of the culprits who are to blame.

I have written about the usual suspects before, but have said little about Hal Borland. I discovered his work not too long ago, and it was clearly a case of "better late than never." I've found a voice in his essays that, although deeper and more perceptive than mine, has a timbre and message I hear in my head whenever I am writing about the land, the trees, and the seasons.

Ten years or so ago, Joanie and I wandered through an auction in town that was trying to rid itself of an old friend's last possessions.

Among Wilbur Hickman's woodworking tools and birdhouses, his coffee cups and old magazines, I found Borland's *Homeland*, a collection of essays that had been written throughout the mid-1960s but printed in book form as the decade came to a close. Wilbur's second-edition hardback copy cost him $4.50; I got it for two bits, and I think it has served both of us well.

Harold "Hal" Borland was born in 1900 near the tiny southeastern Nebraska town of Sterling. I wish I had known that fact when my wife and I were not so far away visiting Willa Cather's place a few summers ago, for I would hope he is celebrated there in some way, although I doubt it.

By the time he was 15, Borland was living in Colorado, both parents ankle-deep in ink at their own weekly newspaper in the small town of Flagler. Despite originally wanting to attend college to be an engineer, Borland eventually studied journalism and graduated from Columbia in 1923 with a degree in literature. Skip forward a decade and a half and Borland was well into a prolific writing career, penning short stories and poetry, biographical and western novels, a variety of non-fiction, and even a play. Perhaps his most famous book came in 1956: *High, Wide, and Lonesome*, which tells the story of his early life on the Plains and growing up as a homesteader. I plan to read it someday.

But what I am most thankful for, and have been most inspired by, are what he came to call his "outdoor editorials," short essays that first ran in the "New York Sunday Times" in 1942. By the time he and his second wife had moved to a 100-acre farm in Connecticut, Borland had written well over a thousand of them; he was still writing for the "Times," and contributing to a few other newspapers when he died in 1978.

Borland wrote with the eye of a scientist and the voice of a poet. He said that he was not "a first-draft writer," that his editorials often underwent half-a-dozen rewrites. He estimated that he spent four or five hours at his typewriter nearly every day of the year, for he couldn't "think the way I want to in longhand."

Some of Borland's patience may be rubbing off on me these days, for I sense I am intentionally slowing down, not because of arthritis or a noticeable change in dimwittedness, but because I have learned to allow things to soak in a bit more, to pay attention to the wind and moon, and to the voices of frogs and the faint whisper of snowfall.

In October 1965, Borland wrote: "Today's daylight will be three minutes shorter than yesterday's. The rising sun in the maples made a dazzling glow, and at noon the light beneath those trees will be more golden than the sunlight itself. Yet within another week or ten days those yellow leaves will fall and rustle along the road in the breeze, and I can stand beneath those trees and see the gleam of stars forming the great square of Pegasus almost overhead."

It is November in the here and now, and I am nearly a thousand miles and over 50 years away from Borland and that old typewriter of his. Yet, I walked my walk tonight and watched my breath as it misted a bit of the air around me. As I loped along, I saw what was left of the sun sliding below the horizon to the southwest; it was barely 6 o'clock.

Along the wood line I saw four deer picking through the corn stubble of a field combined a few weeks ago, and through now-bare branches, I saw slivers of lavender and pink sky fade to dark blue. I haven't noticed those leafless limbs for a good while, because up until a week or so ago they were dressed in sassafras red and hickory yellow.

Borland wrote in the introduction to *Sundial of the Seasons*, a compilation of his nature pieces in 1964, "I am sure that as editorials they have solved no political crises, swayed no elections, and had no noticeable effect on the tax rate and never averted or even eased international tensions…they were written to suggest a somewhat longer sense of time and a different perspective than are prompted by the daily headlines."

So it goes with me, too.

HORNETS' NEST STAYING PUT THIS WINTER
December 12, 2017

Coughs and colds came to visit my family last week, and although I mostly complained about being sick, my wife actually was. So, with her tucked into bed, hacking away in misery, I plopped myself into a recliner with one eye on the Sunday morning news programs, the other closed.

By early afternoon, my back had had enough of the chair, and my stomach enough of the political bickering. In a moment of nose-blowing clarity, I remembered a bit of advice my grandfather often dispensed: that the best way to feel better when ailing was to get out of the house and breathe fresh air. Since it was shirt-sleeves weather, and I was amply fueled by the leftover pumpkin pie I'd uncovered in the refrigerator, I went to walk the woods a while.

After I had descended to the old railroad grade below our place, I wished I had worn hunter orange, for it is now deer season, and I wanted no trespassing marksman to end up posing with my carcass on his favorite social media site. I chose to stay within yelling distance of the house.

As already described in last month's fall feature, I discovered—just after the leaves had begun their autumn decline—a relatively low-hanging hornet nest not far from the house. I had walked past the nest's well-camouflaged hidey hole all summer, never knowing that I had been precariously close to a live hive of bald-faced hornets (*Dolichovespula maculata*). As late as mid-October, I was still seeing them feverishly hovering just outside the bottom entrance to the nest, so the long arm of a zoom lens took me as close to their home as I wanted to be.

Typically shaped like a conga drum, and about a foot wide by nearly two feet in length, the hive was probably loaded with no fewer than 100 hornets, and perhaps as many as 400. As if their name is not enough to scare anyone with the good sense I believe I had in giving them a wide berth, bald-faced hornets' reputations and stings will quickly convince any nitwit who violates their personal space. Not usually aggressive unless provoked, they can hit a target like lightning, and since they have smooth stingers, they can do it again and again, then come back for more.

Retired Ohio naturalist Jim McCormac, now an excellent photographer and blogger, not only knows what a bald-faced hornet's sting feels like, he's watched their behavior for years, most often from a very respectful distance.

"Bald-faced hornets bushwhack, kill, and eat yellow jackets. Now, that is one tough insect: terminators of the wasp world. If the adult hornet doesn't make its own meal of the yellow jacket, it chews it to a pulp and feeds it to young hornet larvae back in the nest," Jim says.

He added, however, that we should simply leave the hornets—which are actually wasps—be, for they are usually "quite mild-mannered, insofar as people go. Leave them alone, and they'll not mess with you either," he adds.

The nest I found is a ragged-looking thing now, for we've had enough freezing temperatures to kill off its occupants; only fertilized queens survive our winters, most often, as Jim reminds us, in "ground burrows or tree cavities." If they were still at home, I think they would have mended their siding by now.

Bald-faced hornets, like the more often-seen paper wasps—who build under our eaves and around our outside light fixtures—create their hives by gathering and chewing wood fibers, then mixing it with their starchy saliva. The nearly-decorative paper they produce is wound around a core of hive cells that are protected deep inside. The nests are collected as works of art, admired as feats of engineering, and sold as decorative collectibles; they are considered to bring good fortune, although I have no idea why. Those who collect the hives will often give them a coat of polyurethane or lacquer, for it doesn't take much to eventually shake their paper to pieces, one layer at a time.

Because my aunt and uncle had a nest hanging in their breezeway for years—harvested from a massive beech tree that sat across from our house—I've always admired their design and construction. I already have three nests hanging around my home, but the one I found this fall will be left alone to fall apart over the winter.

This nest isn't but 15 feet off the ground, which is quite low by folklorist's standards. Long used to predict the depth of winter snows, I am glad that I have found no other hives hanging higher, for they have been spotted well over 60 feet up. And, since I have no intention of tempting the fates with either a blizzard or a sting from a particularly hardy hornet, there it will stay.

A CONSERVATIONIST BEFORE HIS TIME
December 10, 2017

I realize as much as anyone that it is nearly winter. The orange slice of a sunset to the southwest and the brisk north breeze that coursed through my shirtsleeves on my way to the barn this evening have already reminded me of

This Old World

what's ahead of us for the next few months.

Yet, I have no problem at all in sitting at my desk and recalling the itch and green of the wet Wisconsin woods that my traveling companion and I experienced this past July. The memories of that day have prompted me to tell you about our visit to Aldo Leopold's place; perhaps it will warm your cold feet a bit as we face the longest days of the year.

There are some things we have to see for ourselves to make them real, and since my college days, I have wanted to see Leopold's "shack," the one-time cow and chicken shed made famous by what the man did nearby: scribble many of the observations and notes that led to his classic conservationist manifesto, *A Sand County Almanac*.

Leopold had barely finished the book when he died at 61 in the spring of 1948; it was published posthumously less than a year later. I picked up *Sand County* in my first year or two of college, which was about the time that more people were becoming aware that the planet was being eaten one forest, one marsh, one fencerow at a time; Leopold simply realized it earlier than most.

After a visit with Frank Lloyd Wright in Spring Green, we drove east, then north on Wisconsin state highways 14 and 12 to Baraboo, now a tourist town that sits on the southern border of the famously commercial Wisconsin Dells. But we had no interest in splashing about in a pool or waiting in line for an amusement park ride; a pretty drive out to the Leopold Center—built in its namesake's memory a little over a decade ago—put us in the middle of the woods. It sits along a narrow county pavement called Levee Road.

Born in 1887 in Burlington, Iowa, Aldo Leopold was trained as a forester and spent much of his formative years journaling and sketching the wild world as he observed it. His career with the United States Forestry Service took him first to Arizona and New Mexico, and eventually to Wisconsin. By that time, he was beginning to understand the negative impact that people had on land, and he began to develop ideas about how it—and its animals and plants—could be conserved and managed more efficiently. He was eventually hired by the University of Wisconsin as the country's first professor in the field of wildlife ecology and management.

Married in 1912, Leopold brought his wife, Estella, and four of his five children—Starker, Luna, Nina and Carl—with him to Wisconsin; a fifth child, named for her mother, was born in 1927. By 1935, the family had begun working weekends and holidays on a "worn-out and wasted" farm that sat along the Wisconsin River. Its depleted topsoil had been overrun by wind-blown and flood-deposited river sand, and the treeless and barren landscape enabled Leopold to purchase the 80-acre property for about $8 an acre.

From 1935 to 1946, Leopold and his family planted about 3,000 pine trees a year on the farm, and despite the Dust Bowl-like conditions that claimed nearly all of their

This Old World

seedlings in the first few seasons, the Leopolds managed to turn the property around, much of it helped by Aldo's restoration of its prairielands with the seeds and plants he'd found at other sites that were being destroyed by development. Just a hundred yards or so of walking a path from where we'd left our car on Levee Road, the prairie became visible to us, as did the shack, the only structure left on the property when Leopold purchased it.

Since the farmhouse had burned—all that remained was the foundation—the Leopolds hauled the manure of past years out of the shack and made it livable. The family came to treasure its time away from Madison, enjoying the simple pleasures of a life closer to the land. The outhouse—built by Starker and nicknamed "The Parthenon"—was the only structure added to the property over the years. While studying World History in school for the first time, the youngest Leopold daughter came home to announce, "Did you know there's another Parthenon? And it doesn't look anything like ours!"

It had rained much of the night before and the day of our visit to the shack. Despite slathering on a heavy layer of weapons-grade mosquito repellent at the Leopold Center, I soon discovered that our time wandering the Leopold property was to be paid for in blood, particularly my type, for the mosquitoes left Joanie, for the most part, alone. By the time I had my camera bag on my back, the mosquitoes were on me like a plague of boils, and my swatting and slapping jolted nearly every inch I walked and every picture

Mike Lunsford

I took. The heat of the day climbed toward 90 degrees, but the experience was worth both the welts and sweat.

We hiked under a stand of beautiful pines, past the grassy prairie still dotted by flowers, and inspected the locked cabin, which looks very much as it did when the Leopold Family stayed there. Before dams on the Wisconsin River were built, pictures show flood water running nearly up to the shack, but Joanie and I walked a bit through scrub willows and deep sand to reach the banks of the river, which, despite an overcast sky, still appeared blue and calm. Eventually, the mosquitoes forced us into a hasty retreat, but we paused often as we re-traced our steps and headed back to explore the Leopold Center for a while.

Despite his now-famous "land ethic" and the best-selling book, Leopold's greatest legacy is, perhaps, the lives of his children. That became most apparent to us as we watched videos and looked at displays at the center just a few minutes after driving back from the shack. Four of the five Leopolds lived into their 90s, all following in some way or another in their father's footsteps: Starker became a zoologist and author; Luna, a geomorphologist and hydrologist; Nina, a conservationist and researcher; Carl, a plant physiologist; and, Estella, who is still living, a paleobotanist and conservationist. Together, they formed the Leopold Foundation in 1982, and the center, only three-quarters of a mile from the shack, blooms like a beautiful prairie flower in memory of their father.

One of the "greenest" structures in the country (it is

considered "carbon neutral" and uses 70 percent less energy than other buildings its size), the center was built from stone and wood that came from within just a few miles of the site; 500 of the original Leopold pines were harvested for its construction. Its classrooms, meeting center, exhibits, and trails attract visitors from all over the world, and just west of the building a boulder and plaque commemorate the spot where Leopold died of a heart attack while fighting a neighbor's grassfire. Five redbud trees are planted near the site, each representing one of his children.

As we drove away from the Leopold Center a few hours after we arrived, Joanie and I realized that we could have easily spent our day shopping and working on our tans near chlorinated pool water; we wouldn't have been bothered by a single mosquito.

But, as Leopold wrote in the foreword to his book: "There are some who can live without wild things and some who cannot."

SWAN SONG ON A WINTER'S DAY
January 29, 2018

It is becoming harder for me to love the winter as I once did. The season used to mean sleds and farm pond hockey, snow forts and the scent of my grandmother's coal furnace. In those days, I was ignorant of electric bills and dripping faucets and wind chills; I am keenly aware of all three now.

Yet, I do still play outdoors, proven by a cold

evening I spent with my daughter in late December, just before the worst of the big chill and snow of a Siberian Express came barreling through around Christmas.

Although I had already been in the habit of pulling on my heavy coat and boots and stocking cap on some evenings to head to the woods, it was a pleasant surprise to get an email at work from Ellen, who suggested we should hit the road together as soon as I could get home; she would meet me there. A snowy owl had been seen in Vermillion County, and knowing we both wanted to see one, she suggested it be then.

Snowy Owls are rarely seen south of the Great Lakes, but this has been an exceptional year, an "interruption" in their usual migratory patterns. Spurred on by the gorgeous pictures my photographer friends have posted on social media, I too wanted to get into the act.

It took me no more than 10 minutes to change my clothes, shove fresh batteries into my cameras, and, with Ellen riding shotgun in my truck, head west across the river and north to the seemingly endless fields and fence rows where the owl had been sighted.

Ellen and I both knew our chances of spotting one of the all-white Arctic birds were slim. Despite having some idea of where we were headed—she with binoculars and me with a telescopic lens—we realized the odds were long, even though this winter was giving us the best chance, perhaps ever, of seeing one. Driving gravel-roaded grids and aware that we needed to stay at least 100 yards away

This Old World

from any owl we might come across, we gradually saw the sun dipping lower by the minute. A flash of white at least a half mile from where we drove spurred us into action.

Although we found no snowy owl that evening, just as the sun was beginning to set, we came upon a flock of trumpeter swans as they wandered about in a chisel-plowed field; our growing disappointment was gone.

The Audubon Society suggests that as early as 2020, and definitely by 2050, trumpeters will be harder to find in Indiana for they may not be able to enjoy nearly as many favorable tromping grounds here. By 2080, nearly 70 percent of their winter range will be gone, although the birds have made a remarkable comeback from the days when they were not protected by law. Of course, we knew none of this when we came upon the scene, and so we stood a while near the truck and watched and listened to them.

Only after we were there nearly 20 minutes, did I venture a bit down the road with camera in hand. I could hear the swans mumbling about me, although there seemed to be no real panic in them.

The website for the American Bird Conservancy tells me that the trumpeter once bred widely across North America, but, as is often the case, they were nearly hunted to extinction by the early 20th century. Today, these beautiful things—among the heaviest flying birds in the world at upwards of 35 pounds and the "largest waterfowl species native to North America"—are still under siege by loss of habitat and poisons and wind turbines.

Mike Lunsford

Knowing we were seeing something special—and perhaps the only time we would ever see the swans together—my daughter and I were reluctant to leave, not eager even to go home to the warmth of our kitchen. We wandered south and east until past dark, knowing that even if we lucked upon the snowy owl at the next turn that by then it would be too late to see much more than a blur of white.

A few days ago, and despite drifting snow and sub-zero wind chills caused by a brutal wind that slashed through gloves and scarves like a razor, Joanie and I decided to head into town to run errands. Knowing that at one stop she was going to spend nearly an hour, I took off into more Vermillion County farmland to see what I could see; my camera, as usual, lay in the back seat.

Although I was soon numb-faced and teary-eyed from just a few minutes in the slashing wind, I stood on an icy county road to watch a flock of Greater White-Fronted Geese fly overhead. Not long after, I spied a gaggle of Canada Geese that milled about in the stubble of a glacial cornfield as if shopping, their color barely contrasting the grey snow-blown air. Within minutes, a Northern harrier came manically gliding along, hesitant to land because he had undoubtedly seen me long before I had seen him; I managed only two quick hits on the shutter before he vaporized in the windy gloom.

Just before I decided that I could take no more of the cold, that my frozen fingers and runny nose demanded the comforts of my truck's cabin, I heard the familiar bassoon honk of trumpeters. There were four of them headed from north to south toward a pond, just a speck to me a half-mile down the road. With hardly a flap of their wings, they were out of sight in seconds.

Within a month, I had seen the trumpeters twice; the first time, however, was best, for I had company.

PROVERBS, IDIOMS, AND GRANDPA-ESE
February 26, 2018

I've decided to teach my grandson a new language over the coming months. He is a little past two years old now and chattering away on just about anything and everything, excited that he can communicate with taller people who wear uncomfortable shoes and always seem to be in a hurry.

He has become very opinionated, already quite the expert on dinosaurs, naptime, and just about anything else that comes up.

Just a few days ago he surprised my wife by saying, "Excuse me," as he squeezed himself nearly flat between her (seated on the floor with grandson number two) and the living room sofa, and not more than an hour before he admonished her for saying "hippo," when, of course, any 28-month-old knows it is a "hippopotamus."

He has rather smugly informed us both that Mr. Potato Head and Woody from *Toy Story* cannot share their hats, and one evening last week, he told me that I was "acting silly" as I tossed, more than sat him, in his car seat for his trip back home.

He added, "Love you. Get outta here."

As he grows, and despite my rather limited expertise in languages (I was lucky to pull a C in freshman year Spanish), I plan, as my grandparents did by accident, to teach by example the use of what cartoonist Brian Crane calls "Grandpa-ese," a wonderfully expressive, and alarmingly rare form of English that seems to be dying from lack of use.

My grandparents were simple people; they weren't college educated, nor widely read, or dinner party sophisticates.

They all died well before the internet was revealed to the world, but I have to say that they communicated better than most of the people I now know, and I don't mean in the sense of telling the truth or not.

They certainly said what they meant, but they did it more colorfully, more descriptively than we seem to be able to manage now. They spoke a language more figurative, one often wholly imaginative that isn't employed as much in this era of 140-character tweets or ungrammatical social posts, or run-away political correctness.

My school students may think I'm becoming more addled by the year, for I often slip seamlessly into the language of my grandparents' generation, tossing in the occasional idiom, the random colorful phrase, the intermittent figure of speech. "Let's hightail it to lunch," I might say, or try to convince them that I'm not a "stuffed shirt," or explain that I can't buy into their latest fundraiser because I'm "as poor as a church mouse."

My grandparents used all three of those phrases often and with ease, never explaining, never backing up to re-word; they left it up to me to interpret what had just been said. Of course, I could have "googled it" had there been a Google in those days.

Although I fear that we are much better now of talking "at" one another than talking "with" our friends and families and those on opposite political and social fences, I do take heart that the language we speak continues to evolve, and there remain idiomatic batons that continue to be handed off from one generation to the next.

Ron Baker, professor emeritus of English at Indiana State University, and author of *Hoosier Folk Legends*, and an entire bookshelf of other titles about place names and language, says there is reason to still take heart.

"Language and culture are dynamic. Some old usages and traditions disappear; some seem to hang around forever; and some new ones created by individuals gain currency and become traditional," he says.

"Your students may not know or understand their grandparents' expressions, but their grandparents may not know or understand your students' sayings either. Though they may share some folk groups—ethnic, regional, family, religious, for instance—grandparents and students also belong to other folk groups, including age groups and occupational groups that they don't share, so it's natural that they won't always know or understand one another's speech and sayings."

Although I have to say that I have reason to be a bit less optimistic about our language's future than Dr. Baker—for I snipe away in the trenches of a high school English classroom where students come each year less exposed than ever before to books and words not already in their wheelhouses—I hope the good doctor is spot-on when he says, "I think this [apparent slide in the use of proverbs, idioms, and the like] is largely the result of a movement from an agrarian society to a technological society, from homogeneous villages to subdivisions and city blocks, rather than the result of a devolution of language."

So, I have to say that for my grandsons in the long run, and for my students in the short wind-sprint I have left in my teaching life, they are going to continue to hear that I "am on a wild goose chase;" that I feel about as graceful as "a hog on ice," and that, on occasion, I may "fly off the handle." I have been known to "raise Cain," rub somebody's "fur the wrong way," and create a "fine kettle of fish" too. As I head toward retirement, I just hope I am not "robbing Peter to pay Paul," and that I have a comfortable "nest egg."

Years ago, as I followed my Grandmother Daisy around her house one day as she did her chores, some kooky thing her neighbor had done incited her to say, "Well, of course, she's as crazy as a peach orchard boar." I, of course, had no idea what she meant. Decades later, after both she and her neighbor were long gone, I discovered that her turn of the tongue originated in the Deep South and referred to the pigs turned loose in the orchards after fall harvest; they became intoxicated and unpredictable from eating the fermenting fruit.

I love it when I learn things like that, and I'm sure that at some point when my grandsons and I are roughhousing, you know, horsing around or goofing off with some sort of monkey business, I'll drop it into a conversation.

Pretty cool stuff.

CRAVING FOR CRAYONS CONTINUES...
March 26, 2018

My grandson made no attempt to stay inside the lines as he sat at our kitchen table one day last week scratching away with crayons in a garage sale coloring book.

He employed both hands as he scribbled on blank faces and empty shapes, for he hasn't yet decided whether he is a lefty or not; we're letting him decide that for himself.

I consider his tactile progress remarkable, for just a few months ago he was satisfied to mostly dump his crayons into a heap, meticulously place them back into the box, then spill them again.

He actually tries to use colors side by side on the

paper now, although he loses interest pretty quickly, particularly if there is a book or a plastic dinosaur to be found... or a snack.

Daniel's crayons are mostly "leftolas," the semi-official term for the broken and worn stubs that rattle around in countless boxes and recycled cottage cheese cartons in households all across the country. We always have a fresh box ready for him, although I'm not sure he's old enough to truly appreciate the rapturous scent of opening one yet, nor get the peculiarly satisfying feeling of seeing the sharp and exacting look of new crayons perfectly aligned side by side.

If I had my way, we'd make a bigger deal about March 31, for it is National Crayon Day. On that date in particular, I am sure that aficionados nationwide will be coloring, their tongues held at just the right angles as they go about accomplishing their tasks. Many of those trying to stay inside the lines will be adults.

Crayons, particularly "Crayola" crayons, have a fascinating past; the company was founded as Binney and Smith in 1885, named for two cousins who manufactured paint and chalk. Former schoolteacher, Alice Binney, the wife of co-founder Edwin, actually gave the name "Crayola" to their brainchild by combining the words "craie" (French for chalk) with "ola" (oily). For those interested in a pilgrimage, there is a museum: "The Crayola Factory," located in Easton, PA.

In my school days, the Crayola brand was the most

This Old World

desired—although not the only one available—as we walked the aisles of five-and-dimes in the late summer collecting our school supplies for the upcoming year. By my first day in the classroom, I had a new set of Prang watercolors—its plastic-handled paintbrush yet unsmashed and pristine; a pair of pointless scissors, still shiny and unbent; several yet-to-be sharpened jumbo pencils, still unchewed; and a sharp-edged gum eraser, not yet rubbed across a thousand miles of misplaced cursive.

And, of course, my box of crayons was new too, but there was a pecking order established with crayons in elementary schools in those days. Not unlike automobile purchases among high schoolers now, some children groveled in the dust of the smaller utility sizes of 8's or 16's, while other kids drove their Hummer-sized crayon packs of 48 or 64 to school. It is my understanding that Crayola now offers an ultimate "case" of crayons with 152 colors. I might have needed to see a counselor had a classmate come packing one of those into Miss Casper's second-grade class... I have learned that Crayola also produces "personalized" sets, although for me, I wouldn't have cared for that at all; I usually relegated my crayons to an old cigar box.

As ridiculous as it seems, I have a rather rocky past with crayons, and it doesn't involve a doctor's visit with one shoved into an ear, or dining on them with a side order of white paste. I once took a paddling for having too many black crayons in a junior high school art class after, I guess,

I visited the sacred altar of the supply cabinet one time too many. Apparently, my crayon craving didn't sit well with our rather eccentric teacher; perhaps she suspected I was selling them on the playground. I also endured family ridicule for a botched attempt at crayon candle making years before that, but seeing—and hearing—my dad under our kitchen sink as he replaced a colorfully-clogged drain still gives me flashbacks…

Despite the psychological damage of those two mishaps, the mere scent of crayons still produces good memories. In fact, a Yale University study by William Cain in 1982 claimed the smell of crayons as being in the top 20 most recognized aromas. According to "Mental Floss" writer Jake Rossen—in an article that appeared a year ago this upcoming National Crayon Day—crayons' most-identifiable smell is due to their main ingredient: stearic acid (a derivative of beef fat).

I don't color anymore, unless I sit down with Daniel for an impromptu session in between working puzzles or having a quick wrestle, but perhaps I should. A myriad of sources more than suggests that adult coloring has real health benefits, and not just because it may mean more time spent with grandchildren either. According to the *Washington Post's* Nora Krug, who wrote an article about the growing adult crayon craze last year, coloring books dot best-seller lists and demand bookstore shelf space; 12 million of them were sold in 2015 alone.

Having crayons in hand, according to Krug's

sources, can improve weakened motor skills, help adults heal from mental or physical difficulties, lower stress, and clearly has "meditative effects." The size of the crayon box, I might add, does not enter into the equation, although I'm not sure I could face an adult coloring class without the confidence of a box equipped with a built-in sharpener.

In all, there have been about 200 different colors of Crayolas over the years. One might think that the older the crayon, the less sophisticated the colors' names, but that's not quite true. "Madder Lake Red" and "Golden Ochre" were produced as early as 1903, yet their names do pale a bit by comparison to today's "Mango Tango" and "Bluetiful."

And to think that I took a whipping just to keep a few extra black ones.

NO WINTER LASTS FOREVER
April 9, 2018

What a sluggard spring has been this year. Had I been asked in mid-February, I would have said that its unexpectedly warm days were telling us that winter was leaving town early, but then came a colder, much wetter March.

Less than two weeks ago we had a heavy, sloppy snow, and even yet here in April, we've had flurries and are cooler than in average years; I'm sure it will all even out.

The new season was supposed to arrive on March 20; that was the day of the equinox, and although we all expect and accept the unpredictability of Indiana's weather and its odd comings and goings, at least on that day we could look at the calendar with hope.

Yet, four days later, we were greeted with nearly a half-foot of slush and ice, and the woods below my house, once alive with a carpet of green sprouts and frog song, went gray and silent, as if the weather had thrown itself into reverse.

Just two days after the big snow, I tugged on a few layers of clothes and practically skied down the slopes of my back hillside on size 13 boots.

I had to latch onto branches and roots to stay upright, but once on level, yet soaked, ground, I wandered for nearly four hours, making it back up the hill to my back steps just as the rare blue sky of the day was handing itself over to an early-evening rain shower.

Those clouds proved to be the portents of yet another wet week, and as I write this, my cabin window looks out to the north and east at acres of flooded bottom land.

Spring arrived that day in the woods, though; I could tell as a silent mist rose from the cold ground into the warming air. I remember standing quiet and still for a few minutes to watch a painted turtle as it scaled a rotting gray log; it climbed out of our pond's frosty muck to feel the sun on its chilly shell. Later in the spring, I will see a dozen or more turtles at once in that very place.

I also saw, for the first time since late last summer, a

dozen or so plump little phoebes, their white-yellow bellies standing out as they perched on the starkly bare limbs of dead trees that were poking through brown, brackish water. Phoebes are flycatchers, and as I moved closer to them, I wondered what they could be finding to eat just then, but I soon knew, for it didn't take long to walk into a cloud of gnats hovering just a few feet above my already-wet feet. What an oddity to swat gnats and stand in snow at the same time.

Everywhere, I saw greening briars and swelling saplings, all in contrast to the thinning white blanket that was disappearing by the minute; it seemed as though I stood at the very place where a sign post designating spring's birth had been driven into the mud.

The wind, from the north and east when I began the adventure, subtly shifted, and I suspected that by the time I stood again at the top of the hill, it might be coming from the south. Instinctively, I pulled off my cotton gloves and stuffed them into the back pocket of my blue jeans, and within minutes I had to shed one of my shirts too. I left it hanging from a cottonwood branch that I knew I'd pass on the way back home.

I soon spooked a dozen or so wood ducks that had been motoring about in a shallow pool of run-off water; I had no time to even turn a camera their way for they had seen me before I had seen them, their odd-looking green and white and black-helmeted heads too-far gone to see close-up, even through my viewfinder.

A half-hour later, I flushed a blue heron loose from his frog-gigging spot. He had been wading behind a stand of willows, and I didn't see him until he too was as good as gone.

Reddish spear-headed sprouts of skunk cabbage surprised me nearly as much as the birds. I found myself standing amid dozens of the plants, knowing they had been pushing their way up through the snow, even on nights when it was well below freezing. Skunk cabbage is a "thermogenic" plant, producing a little of its own heat, as well as the odor that gives it a name. By the time the trees above it are showing off tiny leaves, those plants will be a foot tall, their exotic deep green leaves appearing nearly tropical amid still-brown grasses and reeds.

On the way back to the house, I came upon a patch of tiny flowers called "harbinger of spring," also known as "pepper and salt." They are among the very earliest flowers of the new year, and I only saw them on my return trip because the snow that had covered them as I went down into the woods had melted away by the time I was headed back out. It is hard to believe that in a few states these flowers are "endangered" or "threatened," for they were everywhere along the path I walked.

As I knocked the mud from my boots at my back step—without a phone, my watch left on the desktop beside it—I hadn't realized how long I'd been gone. I was tired, for I had sat for no more than 10 minutes on a wormy log, thirsty because I had been too lazy to take a bottle of water along, and a little leg weary after climbing the last steep leg of the trip.

Thanks to a house-cleaning friend, I have a new-old book by one of my nature-writing favorites, Hal Borland. In it, he wrote some 50 years ago that "No winter lasts forever; no spring skips a turn." Of course, he'll be proven right.

GRANDSON'S CURIOSITY A GOOD THING
May 7, 2018

A young teaching friend of mine stopped in after school the other day. I am in the process of cleaning out four decades of the heap I call my classroom, and I had promised her a stack of record albums for her collection. It took her no time at all to notice the desktop pictures of my two grandsons, and before long she had her phone out and was scrolling through snapshots of her two little ones.

Eye rolls aside, I think it is a genetic disposition for grandparents to tell stories about their children's children. There is a sense of near-immortality that grandchildren give us, and I already have a collection of stories about my older grandson (our younger one is just 9 months old) that I can call upon when smiling is a hard thing to do.

For instance, we had to bribe him with cookies to get him to leave the woods with us last week. We tried the old, "We're leaving now, and you'll have to find your own way home" routine, but he knew we wouldn't abandon him to the turtles and gnats and horsetails of our pond, so he took his sweet time in tagging along.

Mike Lunsford

Although he's not smiling right now, my son is working on a little project that his firstborn created out of curiosity. Now amidst the "terrible twos," the little guy is at an age when he knows just enough to make him dangerous. He is curious and verbal and rough and messy and bossy; he is into, or up to, something every waking minute, which includes prying up the house's heating and cooling vent covers so he can stash toys (in this particular case, a dismembered "Mr. Potato Head") in his own special hiding place.

The problem is, the parts slipped well past arm's reach, and this time, so did a bulky plastic air deflector, which apparently went down the tube before the toys. He also happened to select a spot in the house where the ducts run through a tight crawlspace. A shop vacuum pulled up the plastic pieces, but nothing has reached the deflector, if it is there at all. I have suggested a plumber's snake or hooked wire, but my son is resigned to having to work on his back under the oldest part of his house where a spelunker might feel at home.

"If you have other ideas, let me know," he told me on the phone, his voice weary from a long week. He's busy and tired, but children rarely consider their parents' schedules when deciding to flush something interesting down the toilet or take grape "Kool-Aid" into the living room or throw-up pizza on a nice bedspread.

I did have an idea: I told him that he needed to count to a few hundred, and remember back to the time that he—

my boy, at 4 or so—decided to "help" me by filling the gas tank of my lawn tractor.

At the time, Evan was old enough to venture out of the gate and fence we had behind our house to play with the cats or toss rocks under the roof of our barn or dump the watering can. He didn't really need supervision every minute and was enjoying temporary freedom from wash cloths and stern warnings and large people. We live in the country; our house is a long way from the road, and it was unlikely that he'd walk off into the woods, so we allowed him a bit of space.

Instead of pulling my mower into the barn the night before, I had left it under the extended roof; Evan apparently thought he'd fuel it up for his dad so it would be ready to go the next morning. I wish he had just checked the tires instead, because he filled the tank with dirt and rocks, then shoved a few twigs in for good measure. Whatever it was that went in it, the tank was filled by the time he'd finished. With his mission accomplished he came to the back door for a sandwich.

I am not going to say that when I discovered the mess I reacted like Pa Ingalls or Andy Taylor or Ward Cleaver. Cleaning out the gunk came with complications, including, for that old model, removing the hood and steering wheel assemblies. I was also working on the assumption that dirt had worked its way into the fuel line, so I had to clean it, then remove and clean the carburetor, replace the fuel filter, and, of course, wash the tank out. It took a good while, including additional time to make a trip into town for parts.

My son's work is far from done when or if he recovers the missing bit of plastic. Actually, I suspect the thing is in some other hidey hole that Daniel has already forgotten about; perhaps the refrigerator vegetable crisper. When the duct is opened like Howard Carter getting to Tutankhamun's sarcophagus, all that will probably be there are a few other toys and cobwebs. I suspect Evan will emerge from the dark with nothing but bloodied knuckles and a dirty shirt...

When my daughter found out what her nephew had done, she laughed and said, "The stuff he does... But boys will be boys."

"What do you mean," I said. "Remember the time you fell in the Wabash River looking for rocks? Your aunt and uncle had to hose you off before they'd let you get into their car."

We clean up a lot of messes that our kids make, but hopefully, along the way, we teach them to clean them up for themselves too. I'm glad that my grandson is curious, that secret hiding places and treasure maps and tossing rocks in the pond will be parts of his childhood, like it was for our children, both boy and girl.

Writer Dorothy Parker sure got it right when she said, "The cure for boredom is curiosity; there is no cure for curiosity."

This Old World

HOW DID IT GET SO LATE SO SOON?
June 4, 2018

Although my friends think I should be doing cartwheels in the wake of my retirement from teaching, I've had a few instances of sadness too. An important chapter of my life has closed, and I'll not get to re-read that part of the book.

One of those moments came as I flipped off the lights of my classroom for the last time a few days ago. I was alone at the school and the halls were unlit and the place was silent and cool. I was there to finish cleaning out a room that had become my second home. It, and my thousands of books and crammed filing cabinets and bulging desk drawers and cramped shelves, needed to be cleared for the next teacher to move in. He or she will undoubtedly enter it as young and untested, and every bit as scared as I was in the days I began, when leisure suits were still in, Jimmy Carter was president, and Three Mile Island was still smoldering.

Although I came to enjoy the semi-chaos of a typical school day, the laughter of kids, their slamming locker doors, and the ever-present litany of questions and excuses and rolled eyes, I also loved the school in the quiet times before the students ever tore into the parking lot.

Many a morning, I sat at my desk, a coffee mug in hand, a stack of papers to grade, just enjoying that peaceful time to organize my thoughts, to get my act together. I was, most often, in my room by 6:30 each morning, preparing myself for what was rarely less than a marathon of a work day.

It hit me, pretty suddenly on that last afternoon, when the lights went out, and I stood in the doorway looking at my desk and podium and through the windows to the woods beyond (a real plus for working in a rural school), that I was never going to walk into a classroom the same way that I have—according to an estimate a teaching friend labored with—nearly 45,000 times. That number could actually be higher, though, for I taught a schedule for years and years where we met even more times per day than we do now, but that doesn't really matter now.

It may sound a bit odd, but on that final day I heard the somewhat melancholy line from Willie Nelson's "The Party's Over" playing in my head. It wasn't Nelson's voice, though, but that of "Dandy" Don Meredith, as he crooned a bit near the end of *Monday Night Football* game broadcasts, appropriate for me because I can't really sing. I loved teaching, and I believe I could have passed muster doing it for a few more years.

Even though many of my best friends retired years ago—making me the only person still in the building that was there on the first day it opened—I have made a new generation of friends who helped keep me younger. Some of them actually became my teachers as technology changed or as the Department of Education handed down yet another ridiculous edict or testing program, or as school shootings and social media changed the game from one of desks in straight rows and raised hands to something else altogether. A few others—the ones I called my "neighbors"—kept me on an even keel, particularly on those days when sanity seemed to be a rare commodity.

My calculating friend also said I had well over a million student contacts in my teaching years, and that was just from regular school days. When I begin to think about the thousands of hours I spent practicing in gymnasiums or riding late-night buses, or the times that Joanie and I sat with kids at the symphony or plays, I realize that I can't begin to put a number on such things.

A few nights before my last trip through the hallways, I stood in front of a group of my friends—the oldest now about 80, the youngest in his very first year of teaching. After a bit of good-natured roasting, and several comments that made my eyes water a little, I told a few tales too good not to be re-told, and then fumbled for the one thing I could end the evening with.

I didn't think it would be as difficult as it was. I've made a living by quoting people—Twain and Thoreau, Lincoln and Jefferson—but instead, all that came to mind was something Theodore Geisel wrote as Dr. Seuss: "How did it get so late this soon?"

I have been asking myself that quite a lot lately. How did my teaching life pass so fast? How could I have possibly outlived some of the kids who sat in my classroom? How could I have seen others come back to teach with me or become my administrators, or, happily, turn out to be doctors and carpenters and engineers and mechanics, and great parents, and now, even grandparents?

How can I have possibly been so lucky, so fortunate to have all of these people in my life, even those who grumbled about the work I gave them and my red-inked scribbles and my persnickety classroom rules? How can I thank that many people over all those years?

The lights are out; the door is locked, and the party is over. I have a busy day planned for tomorrow, though, and I'm looking forward to it.

STORIES FROM OUR FATHERS
June 17, 2018

A man is too busy when he suddenly realizes he has forgotten that Father's Day is fast approaching. So overloaded and preoccupied in the past few weeks that I earned a gag gift from a dear friend who has laughed at my recent absent-mindedness, I had a story finished weeks ago for today that has absolutely nothing to do with remembering our dads; I have now remedied that error.

It isn't the anticipation of gifts or a bit of extra time in my recliner that makes Father's Day special to me, but rather that I remember my dad, not as a great man, but as a good one. So, as we honor fathers today, both living and passed, I have a recommendation for you: Watch the film, *Big Fish*, and please, realize that if you are drying your eyes through the closing credits that you have probably been blessed with a father who is immortal, who will live forever, as long as he is kept alive through stories. Like Edward Bloom, the film's often absent but loving father, your dad is to be treasured.

Daniel Wallace, the author of the film-inspiring book, *Big Fish, A Novel of Mythic Proportions* (1998), believes that each of us lives on as long as someone continues to tell our stories. Both the book and film, although in somewhat different ways, remind us of that. In an interview Wallace did as an afterward for the book, he said, "My own father was a charmer and a kind of rover, similar to Edward Bloom in many respects. ... I can only speak for myself when I say that what I most wanted to learn from my father was who he was."

Wallace's dad and mine had similarities. Since he worked away from home on construction jobs, I mostly saw my father on weekends. When he was home, he often spent his evenings bending his knobby elbows at the bar with his buddies, and there was a long list of family gatherings and parties, weddings and graduations that he missed. We didn't do much together and had very little in common, and I can count on both hands the times we spent shooting hoops or tossing a baseball or fishing. But never did I feel my dad was an "absent father," uninterested in what I was becoming or in what I wanted to do. He was just always on the go, always getting in or out of a pickup truck, a few pencils and pens shoved in his shirt's front pocket alongside a notebook filled with numbers and scribbles.

It is ironic perhaps, but the scene from *Big Fish* that

most reminds me of my dad is one of its very last. It comes after Bloom has died, and as guests arrive for his funeral service—among them a circus ringmaster, a giant, a set of Korean twins and a wealthy businessman—his son comes to realize that each of these very real people, although less exotic than in his father's tall tales, loved Edward Bloom and will miss him.

After the minister has finished his say, they all stand in the churchyard sharing stories about Edward, laughing and gesturing and embellishing their accounts with the exaggerated details that make all good stories worth listening to and re-telling for years to come.

I witnessed the same phenomenon. Many of my dad's roughest, most calloused friends, men who were much more comfortable in work boots than in dress shoes, men who shared their stories and beer more readily than their feelings, have told me things about my dad that I had never known, tales of his charity and good heart and strength and silliness. Several of them, in blue jeans and string ties, shared stories at his funeral; a number of them wept as they carried his casket.

If we are fortunate, we can tell stories about our dads today, and if yours is living, tell him what you most remember about him, and those tales will generate smiles; I guarantee it. This is not just a day set aside for cards and perfunctory gifts that will end up in the back of the closet; it is a day for stories that remain relevant as long as they are passed from one generation to the next.

Wallace believes that and through an email note, he told me so: "I cannot imagine a time when telling our stories — the stories of our mothers and fathers and brothers and sisters, our friends—will ever die. This is what we do, every single day, and what we always have done. Even on platforms that seem—and are—superficial, self-congratulatory, and mostly vacuous, by which I mean Facebook, this is what we're doing."

Will Bloom, Edward's often contrary son, finally came to understand his father's greatness, and often, like him, we do the same thing after our fathers are gone; it is my hope that my own grandchildren will know my dad and grandfather, although they will have never met them. That is my responsibility…

As Will says after his dad's death, "A man tells his stories so many times that he becomes the stories. They live on after him, and in that way he becomes immortal."

A SOFT MAPLE AND A HARD PLACE
June 18, 2018

It took 10 years for me to cut a tree down, and even now, I wish it had taken even longer. Not to cut it up, mind you, but to commit to dropping it—a huge silver maple that stood in my front yard.

It has worried me like a nagging tooth for so long that even now I still expect to glance out our living room windows to see it hulking there, its bark peeling, its whirligigs helicoptering to the ground, its roots still anchored in our hardpan clay like a battleship in harbor. I miss it.

When Joanie and I first moved to our place years ago—she, big with our daughter who would be born within days of our unpacking the dishes—the tree was the tallest of a set of soft maple triplets that stood in a ragged line across our front yard.

All three were already tall, and I believe old enough that the man who built our house 20 years before couldn't have possibly planted them for future shade. Rather, I think he chose the spot for the house because the trees were there beforehand, and I can imagine him framing and roofing under a spreading canopy of summer green.

I know silver maples are not desirable trees; my extension agent brother-in-law hates them. They are messy and they split and their fall color most often is an anemic yellow. They drop twigs in the slightest of breezes, develop soft spots at any place they are trimmed, and have disturbing relationships with power outages, mossy shingles, volcanically eruptive roots, and back-breaking leaf piles; woodpeckers and ants are enamored with them.

Over the years, I have planted a gorgeous oak, a nice yellow poplar, and a blazing red maple in my front yard, but I could never bring myself to cut the big old silvers down; I just couldn't do it. I like and respect trees, and since these three were apparently healthy, I wasn't going to touch them despite their flaws. Call it lack of foresight or a case of stupidity, but the rattle of their leaves and their bird nests

This Old World

and their cooling shade endeared them to us.

Nearly 10 years ago, I hired a tree trimmer to shape the maples. I didn't want to "top" them, which isn't recommended anyway, so I had him remove enough interior branches to allow the wind to blow through them. He told me then that the tree in question should probably be taken down.

On a scale, with 10 being the worst shape a tree could be in, he said ours was already about a 7, that it might split at any time, for its massive trunk was supporting two main branches that together were wider than the size of its base. It was only a matter of time, he said, before we would be wearing the tree on our house.

Despite the anxiety I suffered, particularly anytime the wind stiffened in a June thunderstorm or the weatherman was calling for a fast-moving cold front, I persisted in making excuses for keeping the tree. But as this winter gave over to the spring, I knew that the tree's shedding bark in a spot no smaller than a doorway was a warning sign that a split was imminent, that a rotted spot lay just under the surface, and I had better have it brought down.

My long-suffering wife had to have grown tired of my wrestling with the decision; she loved the tree too, but I chattered about it to anyone who would listen. Years ago, we had a swing under it; our kids played around it; our windows opened to the breezes that blew through it; and just last fall, its leaves were inexplicably golden, as pretty as it had ever been.

Yet, it took one man repelling between the branches like a chainsaw-wielding Tarzan, with two more on the ground, to drop it in a single sweaty day. Just like that, a tree well over 4 feet wide at the ground was gone; a relatively small pile of firewood was left for my son's evening camp-outs.

Call me a "tree hugger," but the indiscriminate destruction of trees makes me sick. I know I had to cut the maple to potentially save us both harm and an insurance claim, but there is much we can learn from trees.

I don't believe, as the Greeks did that they deliver prophecies, or that they murmur to one another in some sort of secret language. A fascinating article in *Smithsonian Magazine* this past March captivated me with the new science of trees as conveyed by German forester Peter Wohlleben and Canadian forest ecologist Suzanne Simard. They face criticism for applying human emotions to trees, but to not do that makes us something less than human, I think.

I do believe that living things have the right to stay in place; after all, the silver maple was here before I was. Yes, I mow grass, I pull poison ivy from fence rows, and I cull weeds from my flower beds, but that old tree—all 65 feet of it—reminded me that my outward appearance as I age, does not necessarily mean my usefulness is over, my value diminished. I know that eventually it had to be cut, but whether it was this year or 10 years from now, I couldn't have known. I was stuck between the tree and a hard place.

Over the summer, I plan to have the maple's stump ground away; I will bring in soil and sow grass seed and plant a new tree where the old one stood. I won't plant another like it; right now I am considering a scarlet pin oak if I go large, a flowering crabapple if small. It's the least I can do.

RASPBERRIES IN THE SUN
July 2, 2018

Although common sense suggested another time would have been better, I chose one of the muggiest and hottest days last week to cut weeds along the steep hillside just below my cabin. Feeling restless since I had accomplished little that day, I waded into a stand of head-high sumac and knee-deep poison ivy with a revved-up trimmer in my already sweaty hands.

As if the itch and humidity and deerflies were not irritating enough, it didn't take long to realize that I was going to either have to change to a saw blade or cut some of the tougher-stemmed brush by hand; I chose the latter just because I wanted to get the job done right away then wash myself off at the hydrant.

So, in an already-soaked shirt and sunglasses smeared and steamed by a mop of dripping hair, I hacked away with a double-edged hand cutter, hardly whistling while I worked.

Mike Lunsford

And then I saw the raspberries. They were on just a few stray thorny stems, but I instinctively emptied my hands and began gobbling the berries like popcorn, the familiar sweet-tart juice nearly ambrosia amid that sweltering misery.

Wild raspberries used to grow in abundance along our woods, but despite my trimming efforts, our plants haven't done well over the years.

Joanie used to wander around our place at picking time and always came up with an ice cream bucket or two, more than enough to make a few pies and put up a half-dozen jars of jelly. But encroaching shade or invasive plant neighbors have gradually won out, I guess, and the deer surely beat us to most of what we don't easily see.

I have few more pleasant memories of childhood than those of walking along our pastures or woods, mostly near overgrown fence rows, grabbing raspberries by the handfuls, never waiting to wash the fruit before cramming them into my mouth. No one sprayed poisons much then, at least not there, and it was obvious that I was walking where our farming neighbors rarely mowed, so unless I saw obvious evidence that a bird had visited the plants just before me, I never thought twice about the immediate gratification of eating the berries warm and unwashed. Their juice would often leave my fingers and t-shirts stained, but that was a small price to pay.

What was particularly satisfying was finding a hot spot of ripe berries—always worth wading amidst the weeds and the thorns with an inevitable loss of blood. The berries would easily pull loose from the tough vines and lie in the palms of my hands until I had accumulated a mouthful. A single raspberry, by the way, actually consists of about 100 tiny individual fruits called "drupelets." Each house one of the plant's many seeds; fibrous microscopic hairs keep them knitted together.

By mid-June, my grandmother, aunt, and mother would head out into the dewy mornings, before the heat of the day came up, to pick berries together. Despite my grandfather growing raspberries in one of his two gardens, his harvest was rarely enough, for we were a family of cobbler and pie eaters and canners. So, those three saints, who I rarely saw in pants, would pull on an old blouse, tie their hair up in big blue handkerchiefs, tug on their jeans and old shoes, and hunt for patches of berries as a team.

I never envied their struggles with chiggers and gnats, or the poison ivy and mosquitoes that they fought off at berry-picking time, but I loved the fruits of their labors, particularly when they'd come home with buckets of raspberries, some more ripe and darker purple than others.

In unguarded moments I'd grab a few berries, rarely appreciating the amount of work they put into picking them. Usually within that very day, they'd be in my grandmother's hot kitchen amid bags of sugar and mixing bowls, rinsing the berries and making jelly and jam. The pot of melted paraffin they used to seal the jars was perhaps the most fascinating aspect of the whole process for me.

Mike Lunsford

Wild black raspberries (*Rubus occidentalis*) are just one of many species of raspberries; they have also been called a "thimblerry" or "scotch cap," as well. What I didn't know as I sprinkled them on my morning cereal or evening ice cream was that they are high in fiber, have more vitamin C than oranges, dose us with folic acid, and are actually low in calories (if you don't count the sugar that is inevitably spooned over them).

Raspberries reportedly are effective treatments for joint inflammation and high blood pressure too, and they may have come to the New World from Turkey. One source says that Russia produces more raspberries than any country in the world—125,000 tons a year.

Rosie Lerner, Extension Consumer Horticulture Specialist at Purdue University, says that she's not seeing fewer raspberries in her area at all: "I have more berries on my land as I choose to let them stay, but wildlife usually beats me to the harvest."

Lerner says that she has not seen any evidence that there is a nutritional difference between cultivated and wild types of raspberries. "Certainly, cultivars are usually considerably larger and more disease resistant," she says.

Lerner also added that despite my joy in picking and eating raspberries as I went about my weed cutting, it's always a good idea "…to be sure what, if any, chemicals the plants may have been exposed to. From a food safety standpoint, you should wash the berries first, but, of course, many of us have eaten them straight off the plant. And, be sure adults have correctly identified the plant; we don't want kids assuming all berries are edible."

I'm no Euell Gibbons (yes, he of Post "Grape-nuts" commercials) that looks to eat every root, grub, or leaf he encounters, but finding and gulping down wild black raspberries is surely one of the great simple and surprising pleasures of living the rural life.

And, despite the odd logic, I know they can make cutting weeds on a hot day a bit easier too.

CELEBRATE ERNIE PYLE FOR WHAT HE WAS
July 30, 2018

There is a passage written by Ernie Pyle that has stayed with me for years. It isn't about the brutal frontline fighting in Italy, or the "dogface" infantrymen he dug ditches with, ate with, even died with; it isn't about the terrible costs he witnessed as he walked the sands of Normandy's beaches after D-Day. It is about his mother, Maria, who, after a series of strokes had gradually diminished her, died in March 1941.

"I went alone yesterday to the graveyard, and stood in the sharp wind over my mother's grave, with its flowers put there on a recent day when I was across the ocean. And as I stood there it seemed to me that she and I were all alone in the world, and I could speak to her... It was brief. I could not bear it. I got into the car and put on my dark glasses and drove to town and got a loaf of bread for supper, and drove home with it as though I had not been anywhere special and nothing had happened.

"In whatever mystic form it may have been, we had had our final communion. Beyond that lies only ritual. I will never go again to my mother's grave. Others may not understand why. But she does."

When Pyle wrote those words, the war that was to make him even more famous than he had already become as a roving correspondent for Scripps-Howard News Service was yet to directly involve the United States.

He died in April 1945, killed by a Japanese machine gunner's bullet on the tiny Pacific island of Iejima, and as far I know, never returned to the grave in Bono Cemetery, which isn't far from where he was born near Dana.

This Friday marks the first national Ernie Pyle Day, the 118th anniversary of his birth. He lived just 44 years, and his Pulitzer Prize and Purple Heart and front page columns from the European and Pacific Theatres and his immortal Captain Waskow and his ability to connect with common people all will be mentioned, and rightly so.

But I believe Ernie Pyle was a great writer, not just because he crouched in the mud of foxholes and felt the hot breath of bullets about him and went without a shave and nearly smoked himself to death and left his more comfortable life in the states for a miserable one.

He was a great writer long before the war's first rumbles were wrought by Hitler's goose-stepping troops and Panzer divisions. He drove thousands of miles through and across his own country, telling the stories of everyday

This Old World

Americans who were struggling with the dust and misery of the Great Depression, and he even wrote of his too-infrequent trips back to his home place on the table-flat cornfields of Vermillion County.

Perhaps his very best book is one he never lived to see, a collection of those thoroughly American stories called *Home Country*, which was compiled in 1947, two years after his death.

Phil Hess, the vice president of the Friends of Ernie Pyle, which supports and maintains the Ernie Pyle World War II Museum and Pyle's birthplace in Dana, simply says of the writer, "He was a compassionate observer of the small details of the history of his time...He wrote from the common man's view of the events they were living."

I preached Ernie Pyle's writing to my high school students for years, not because I had to, but because so many of my students knew nothing about him, past the name of a local elementary school. Of course, literature is gradually being crowded out of Indiana's schools these days, and Pyle is just one essential writer who gets passed by; I hope National Ernie Pyle Day helps change that. So does Steve Key, president of the Board for the Friends.

"The Friends of Ernie Pyle have a couple of goals when it comes to sustaining Ernie's legacy with future generations," Key says. "We hope to fund the creation of an educational unit for Hoosier fourth-graders studying Indiana History. He [Pyle] recently was selected as one of the top 10 Hoosiers historically, so he should be included in any elementary history of Indiana. The Friends also would like to fund the development of an educational unit focused on his writing style that could be used by high school English teachers in Indiana or any state," he added.

And what was Pyle's style? The best description I have ever read came from the late Charles Kuralt, who, in the forward to *Ernie's America*, wrote, "We don't see that his pieces are artistic. We do see that they are true."

In another column Pyle had written about returning home, this time before his mom had died, he realized that he had forgotten to get her a birthday present, so he improvised by whittling a piece of wood she could hold in her stroke-withered hand to keep it from being so sore.

The morning after giving her the stick, he was preparing to leave and go on the road again, but was happy to see her still holding the wood. "Do you know what?" she asked him.

"No, what?" he replied.

"And then she laughed a while before she could speak, and finally she stopped and reached out for my hand, and said, seriously, 'Some of these days you're going to die. And when you do, the world will get along just fine without you. Do you know that?'"

The world has gone on, now years and years after Pyle's death. But to read his work—the wonderful simplicity of his writing—is something to be remembered for a long time.

THE GOOD OF SIMPLE TECHNOLOGY
August 13, 2018

I'm not sure why I waited until mid-day, but I grabbed a hoe last Saturday and walked out to where my lawn reaches the road. I don't like to see the weeds grow in the gravel between the pavement and the grass, so I often just take a few minutes to walk along and nip them in the bud. It just so happened that I decided to do it on a day when the sun was throwing hard rights to the top of my head, and sweat was in my eyes in minutes.

The hoe is a wonderful piece of single-function technology. It was invented with just one thing in mind; when, and by whom, I have no idea, but surely it is nearly pre-historic. The particular tool I used that day was already very old when my mom gave it to me over 30 years ago. I believe she said it was her grandmother's, and it has been honed so often that its blade is ground away at its edges; it's at least an inch or two shorter than when it was new, well over a century ago. It may sound impossible, but I am almost certain the original handle—probably hickory or oak—is still in it.

I use that hoe because I have never found one better; the steel in new blades now can't hold edges like the old ones, and even if I bought a brand new one, I don't think it could serve its purpose nearly as well. We live in an age of built-in obsolescence, but my hoe could still be doing its job another hundred years from now. I have at least three others because I keep thinking it will eventually break. My second-favorite is one I bought at auction, and it had to have been forged during the Truman administration.

A can of weed killer would do the job near the road without much of an investment in energy—I know that. I primarily use a homemade concoction of vinegar and salt and soap for weeds that is environmentally safer, but spraying doesn't quite give me the satisfaction of getting to the root of the problem. Besides, it wasn't worth making a batch when I could be finished with the job in 10 minutes with my hoe. Tools like hoes reduce the confronted issue to its lowest denominator: man vs. weed, for instance. I am not looking to create work for myself, but since I didn't pay a dime for the old tool, I can say that with a little effort I probably saved much more than that.

A few years ago, I listened to education expert Ken Robinson on a "Ted Talk" in which he said his daughter had told him that his wristwatch was a single-function technology. He said that she—an entire younger generation, actually—no longer wears wristwatches because iPhones and tablets and exercise trackers serve more purposes than simply giving the time of day. As you probably suspect, I still wear a wristwatch myself, but since it also keeps the date and has a stopwatch in the tiny window below its sweep hand, I consider it a step above the hoe, technology-speaking. It's waterproof too ...

A news story a few days ago reminded me of how my generation, like all others, eventually gets caught between technological shock waves. It was announced that

This Old World

Apple was the first company in history to reach a net worth of $1 trillion, and the iPhone was primarily responsible; it has re-defined technology. I use one myself; however, despite it being just a few years old, some people find it laughably outdated. I once read that one early-generation iPhone had more computing capability than all the computers used by NASA to put man on the moon, yet I can carry it in my back pocket.

It may have been the hoe that originally got me going with this line of thinking, but as I watched an old movie the other night—it being stored for months on my DVR (an inconceivable thought just a few years ago)—I revisited the idea again. A character was using a pay telephone—you know, a glass booth with a hinged door—to make a call. I remember always keeping change in my pocket for that very purpose. I'm not sure I can find a public telephone now, and usually the only change I have on me is what I've found in a parking lot, a dropped penny or two.

But don't discount the value of single-function technology. When I think about what my friends Joe and Dennis and Bill can create with wood chisels and sandpaper and paint brushes, with wood and clay and paint, my respect for things hand-held and unplugged increases. It is the skill that turns the wrench, that drags the bow across the violin's strings, that measures twice and cuts once that deserves admiration, perhaps more so than being able to merely push a button.

Years ago, my grandfather often walked down the hill from his house to ours on early summer mornings to drag me out of bed to tackle some job he thought I'd like doing at less than minimum wage. For a few weeks every summer, we hoed young strawberry plants for a farmer near town, and I realized then that my grandpa could outwork any man I knew.

We'd start as the heat of the day was building, staring down impossibly long rows, and we'd clean the weeds from around the tender plants. He handled his hoe like a surgeon's scalpel, and within just a few minutes I could look up and see him shrinking in the distance as he motored through his work as if paid by the plant; on occasion, he'd stop to swipe a whetstone he kept in his pocket across his hoe's blade, then get back to it. He sometimes reached the end of his row and met me in the middle of mine coming back, his sleeveless undershirt soaked, his forehead speckled with the sunlight through his wide-brimmed straw hat.

In the years since, I've done a little hoeing myself, but I think I'm still impressed by that memory as much as I am by anything my iPhone can do.

A DAY AT THE BRANCH
August 26, 2018

It has stopped raining as I write this—at least for a while. Since yesterday afternoon, we have seen a few gentle inches fall, and the winding creek near us is muddy and has

This Old World

risen a bit. The wandering finger of a branch on my in-law's small Parke County farm is running again too, pointing what is has to offer toward the Big Raccoon.

We were surprised to see any water between the branch's banks when we took our oldest grandson for a walk there a few weeks ago. The month had not provided much rain, and the day we chose promised us nothing but mosquito bites and damp clothes, but off we went anyway, if anything, to get out of the house and pick up rocks and breathe air filtered through maple and cottonwood leaves.

Daniel loves the outdoors, and we have built a special kinship with him as we've walked and waded and wandered about. To know that we have just begun this journey with him and that he is now old enough to speak to us and ask questions is a great reward, for we are country people who want our grandchildren to have lives shared with nature, as ours have been.

The branch was running, and in some bends, we even sank in the cool and clear water to our shins. It gurgled over sand in some places, and stumbled over and around large stones in others. Although it takes just a few rainless weeks to stop the stream in its tracks, a half-dozen or so springs feed it just enough to keep the water striders and minnows reasonably happy most of the time.

Yet, it isn't all that unusual to find it little more than a narrow west-to-east ditch that lazes out of the woods between two cornfields, bone-dry and lined with milkweed and mullein and Johnson grass in the places where the sun can reach it all day. In the rainy springs or wet summers, we have seen it rise three or four feet in the matter of a few hours, and it is hard to believe that such an ordinary place can be so unpredictable, even dangerous. This year, we have seen more sunchoke along the branch, and swallowtail and monarch butterflies flit in the heat to get a taste of it and brown-eyed Susans and Queen Anne's lace.

It was mid-morning by the time we got to the branch, and the sun was pushing the temperatures toward the uncomfortable when Daniel, wearing new rubber boots and a ball cap, jumped into the water. We headed upstream behind him under a canopy of trees that soon swallowed us.

With our feet in the water, we were cool enough that we spent several hours just seeing what we could see, and that was plenty.

Walking like shaft miners in some places, Joanie and I stooped under low-hanging branches, stopping to push blackberry briars away here and there, listening to our grandson chatter about spider webs, horsetails, and fallen trees.

The birds had gone silent in the heat, and in some places we had to hoist Daniel over limbs that were too high for him to scale. But usually, what he couldn't walk under or around, he climbed over himself, and within an hour we were far enough back into the woods that we feared he'd never make the return trip under his own power. Only our empty bellies persuaded us to turn around.

Although it is unlikely that Daniel will recall these

days, we know we are introducing him to the woods—and, yes, that includes the occasional bug bite and weed itch, the inevitable scratch or fall and sweat-soaked shirt—because we think it is good for him, and for us.

There is plenty of scientific data available that supports the idea that children who spend time outdoors are the better for it. Collin O'Meara, the president and CEO of the National Wildlife Federation, recently cited numerous arguments in The Washington Post that kids who regularly spend time outside sleep better, have improved eyesight, are more creative, and have stronger bones than children who, unfortunately, fall into the new average of sitting "five to eight hours a day in front of a digital screen."

We are determined that that scenario not be the case for Daniel, but our interest goes even deeper. It is our hope that he will develop a love for the natural world, that he has a respect for all living things, and above all, that he grows up with an undying inquisitiveness that is enacted by looking closely at things, such as those we saw that day: a huge dark fishing spider that walks on the surface of the branch to catch its prey; a beautiful female box turtle that could be a half-century old; a freakish growth I am told is "plasmodial slime mold;" a giant cottonwood tree; a jewel-winged damselfly; a snail clinging to a head-high stand of pigweed; a green darner shining in the sun; half-dollar sized bits of gneiss and schist that have washed down from the hillsides... We hope his first impulse is to protect that which we now know is not limitless or never-ending; some may disappear before Daniel is our age.

A month ago, my family took a trip to Michigan. Although shopping is not my idea of amusement, I found myself in Black River Books in South Haven. Against my better judgment, I left a used copy of Sigurd Olson's *The Singing Wilderness* on a shelf, convinced I already had the book at home. I didn't, and have forgotten to whom I've loaned it.

Olson was a true adventurer and paddler and hiker; he was a fine writer too. In that book he wrote, "Joys come from simple and natural things; mist over meadows, sunlight on leaves, the path of the moon over water."

A morning spent with your grandson can be added to that list. One can do worse than to be an inspector of locust thorns, water-tumbled rocks and footprints left in the mud of a branch.

SOMETHING MAGICAL ABOUT SUNFLOWERS
August 27, 2018

I found a gang of small sunflowers growing together in an old whiskey barrel planter near my barn early this summer; they were pale and weak-looking things that appeared doomed.

Rather than pull them to make room for the usual coleus we plant there, I dug them out in a single scoop and transplanted them to a concrete planter that sits near our door; ironically, the planter is adorned with the smiling face of a friendly sun.

This Old World

No doubt the offspring of seeds a careless cardinal or speeding sparrow accidentally dropped in the soil, the plants were growing in a spot that was too shaded for them to prosper. They are now well over a yardstick tall and blooming brightly, so I'm happy that I gave them a chance to do their thing.

There is something magical about sunflowers. Rough as sandpaper, laden with bees and beetles of all sorts, and seen growing as perennial natives in roadside ditches and as annuals in gardens, flower boxes, and fields, one would think they are so common that we'd hardly notice them. But they make us smile, and for that reason alone merit our attention.

I have written before about "sunchoke," a wild sunflower, also called Jerusalem's artichoke, earth apple, and sunroot. It is just one of about 50 varieties of sunflowers, all native to our hemisphere, that were often cultivated at one time or another by Native Americans. Sunchoke's main attraction is its roots, not the seeds we leave for the birds and squirrels or shell and spit by the truckload at ball parks.

With the recent growth in the popularity of towering mazes, colorful hybrids with deep red and bright orange petals, and home décor items that dress-up living rooms and patios, sunflowers seem to be everywhere.

For instance, friends of ours have planted an entire front yard in sunflowers this year. The acre-wide patch is just up the road from us, and I headed that way one sweltering day last week, willing to accept the heat and itch for a chance to see them as their colors peaked in summer's homestretch.

Cheri and Rick Peacock, who loaned their children and grandchildren to me to teach, head a southern Parke County farming operation; Cheri was our school corporation's treasurer for 34 years. Both are happy with the decision to plant sunflowers.

"Rick didn't want to mow the hill [in front of their house]," Cheri says. "We talked about hay or soybeans, which is what he planted last year, but sunflowers were different. He's certainly kept people wondering what he's going to plant these past several years."

Besides a front yard filled with color, the Peacocks have enjoyed watching the reactions of passersby. "People have been curious, and we've seen slow-moving or stopped traffic when they drive by and see them," Cheri said. "I saw a group of bicyclists stop and take pictures, and we had a photographer take some senior pictures in them this past week. Knowing that others seem to be enjoying them as much as we do has been a pleasant surprise."

Despite blooming well before the summer is finished, sunflowers, nonetheless, direct our attention toward fall. We see their cousins along the roads—mostly black and brown-eyed Susans—as the crickets and katydids begin to sing their final summer arias.

All sunflowers belong to the aster family and the genus, *"helianthus"* (a literal Greek translation of the name). Europeans who came to North America during the Age of Exploration found them already cultivated by the native peoples who often crushed them and used the oil for cooking and dressing hair, and for making flour. According to the Lady Bird Johnson Wildflower Center, Native Americans also used the flowers for yellow and black dyes, and another source noted that by the 19th century, some people believed sunflowers planted near their doors warded off malaria through their strong scent.

Each sunflower is actually 1,000 to 2,000 tiny flowers growing together in one bed of seeds. I see the goldfinches, most often perched upside down, tugging away at the smallest of them, an exhausting exercise after the relative ease of stripping the pin-like seeds of coneflowers and bull thistles; mourning doves love them too, although they most often feed on what has been dropped.

Because of this year's results, the Peacocks plan to plant sunflowers again next summer. Cheri says that although this was the first year Rick planted them on the hill in front of their house, he planted the flowers about ten years ago at the edge of a field just for the birds. She added that a second planting looks better than the first, and said, "The number of bees on them was a surprise to us. We expected birds, especially the yellow finches."

Although I haven't taken notice myself, it is said that young sunflowers track the sun's daily progress, an activity called heliotropism. Some may believe it folklore, but there is science that says otherwise. Research suggests that the flowers turn as their stems elongate and grow as each day wears on. Only when sunflowers grow old do they stay still and face the east for good.

The poet, Mary Oliver, wrote of sunflowers: "...each of them, though it stands/in a crowd of many,/like a separate universe,/ is lonely,/the long work of turning their lives/into a celebration/is not easy..."

For that reason alone, we need to appreciate the sunflowers while we have them.

BROTHERS IN ARMS
October 8, 2018

It has become a habit for me to take my camera for a walk in the evenings. The light is low, and the early fall weather and changing colors have made me want to wander a bit in the hours before sunset.

A few weeks ago I found myself in Mount Pleasant Cemetery, a pretty southern Parke County graveyard near no place in particular. I have written about Mount Pleasant before; several friends who wish to be buried there have prepared their markers, and several more, already passed, patiently wait for them there.

Mount Pleasant is nearly always shaded, bordered to the east by sassafras that will soon be brilliant orange, to the west and south by parchment-dry cornfields and weedy fencerows, and to the north, by a grove of black locusts and deep, cool ravines.

The grass had just been cut as I walked between

This Old World

rows of Browns and Huxfords and Baldridges, and I came upon, as I often have, a gravestone that made me pause. It was that of George W. Dixon, born in January 1845, dead in 1863 at just 18.

Although his was not a military marker, the inscription on the stone made it clear that he served in the Civil War, proclaiming him a "Soldier of the Union." Dixon's unit was Company C of the 71st Regiment of the Indiana Volunteers.

Of course, I immediately wondered if he had been killed in battle, and knew I would do a little research to find out.

But before I could think much about Dixon, I caught sight of a familiarly-shaped military headstone, slightly askance and framed by yellowing iris blades and a small and fading American flag.

The grave was that of another veteran of the War Between the States, Allen Baugh, who served in Company C of the 19th Kentucky Infantry; there was no birth or death date given for him, and the hint of a story behind his marker, and why he was where he was, intrigued me just as much as discovering what had happened to Dixon.

Parke County has a tempestuous past when it comes to the Civil War. Indiana was, after all, a state partially settled by people who had migrated northward, as my family had, from North Carolina and Virginia, Tennessee and Kentucky. There was considerable sympathy toward the Southern cause in the years leading up to and during the war, and on occasion, emotions boiled over into violence, including a shooting between two rival factions in Rockville in 1862; local elections during the time were always hotly contested.

Parke County Historian Randy Wright said of the time period: "It seems that most of those living in Parke County were strong supporters of the Union, but there were a few Copperheads, and there are tales of shootouts between them and those that supported Lincoln."

For that reason alone, I suspected that Baugh may have gone south to serve with the Confederacy. After all, I have spotted at least one other gravesite of a former Rebel soldier in another county graveyard about a year ago. But that was not the case at all, nor did Dixon probably die in battle.

Dixon's unit organized in Terre Haute in July 1862, leaving the state from Indianapolis in mid-August for Lexington, Kentucky; it was soon involved in action at the Battle of Richmond on August 29-30, a crushing Confederate victory. According to National Park Service records, the unit was "mostly captured, paroled, and sent back to Indianapolis," not an uncommon practice during the war. The 71st quickly re-organized and headed to Kentucky again just after Christmas, training at Muldraugh's Hill, perhaps under William Tecumseh Sherman. Later, the unit was, once again, captured and paroled, and by the time it was back in Indianapolis, it re-organized into the 6th Indiana Cavalry and was on its way to heavy fighting in

This Old World

Tennessee and Georgia by February 1863. But Dixon wasn't with them.

Although he may have been wounded—there is no indication of it—Dixon died in Indianapolis, speculatively of one of the many diseases that ravaged Civil War era camps: influenza, typhoid, measles, tuberculosis….

Baugh was the youngest of three brothers from Highland, Kentucky, who signed up to fight in the war in the critical border state. Born around 1842, his hometown was so contentious over the causes of the war that, according to a family biographical site posted by Priscilla Claypool, the local Methodist church had to use two doors to keep the factions apart.

Described as being about 5'10" with light hair and blue eyes, Baugh fought at the Union victory at Cumberland Ford and was then involved in the Battle of Perrysville; by December 1862, he was hospitalized and eventually given a medical discharge. Returning home after the war, Baugh married in 1870 and moved to Hillsdale, Indiana, then traveled on to Kansas, came back to Kentucky, then again headed to Indiana after separating from his wife. He purchased property in Florida Township in southern Parke County, and died at just 44. Claypool notes that Baugh instructed one of his daughters—Minnie Bell—that the name of his military unit was to be inscribed on his gravestone.

There were more Baughs buried at Mount Pleasant, so I returned a few days ago and found them. None of their gravestones bore the names of Allen Baugh's children, who, like their father, must have been restless and on the move before their deaths.

But not far from the two Union soldiers' graves, I found a stone for Michael and Lydia Dixon Baugh. Michael died in 1895 and Lydia in 1914; both outlived and are buried with all four of their children. One was named George; he was born in 1863, perhaps named for an uncle or cousin who died in that same year.

It appears that Allen Baugh and George W. Dixon, eternally separated by just a row or two of gravestones and who fought in a great war, may have been more than just brothers in arms.

A DAY WASTED PROBABLY ISN'T
October 22, 2018

There is an often-told story about the grandson of the 2nd president, John Adams.

Charles Francis Adams, a state senator, United States Congressman, and ambassador to Great Britain during the Civil War, meticulously kept a diary, and encouraged his seven children to do the same.

"A diary is the Time Piece of life," Charles's father, 6th president, John Quincy, once wrote, "and will never fail of keeping Time, or of getting out of order with it."

Charles learned the lesson well, and abhorred wasting time, even going so far as to describe a day in which he'd taken one of his sons, Henry Brooks Adams,

This Old World

fishing.

"Went fishing with my son," Charles wrote. "…a day wasted."

Of course, you probably know how the story goes: The boy described the day in his own diary as, "Went fishing with my father today — a most glorious day."

I have often wondered what perspective my own children—and now, grandchildren—will have on the days we have spent together; I hope they never felt I was bored as we tromped off to a pond or wandered the woods, drove highways on family vacations or played board games while the snow fell outside.

It has taken much of a lifetime for me to realize that "wasting time" may be a virtue rather than a sin, although I have always suspected it.

Years of work that involved calendars and deadlines and due dates have made me fidgety and chronically rushed, even now, when there is little need for it. My Puritan work ethic makes me feel guilty—and in my wife's case, even more so—when I while time away accomplishing little.

I am personally working on the habit of wasting more time, or rather, re-evaluating what the term even means; I think it might be a long rehabilitation process. But, at least some of my therapy has come in the form of Alan Lightman's interesting little book, *In Praise of Wasting Time* (102 pages; Simon & Schuster; 2018).

Lightman is Professor of the Practice of Humanities at the Massachusetts Institute of Technology. A physicist and novelist, he believes that each of us has a duty to ourselves to spend quiet time alone every day, and he worries that much of humanity has become "...so crushed by our schedules, to-do lists, and hyper-connected media that we no longer have moments to think and reflect on both ourselves and the world..."

I believe Lightman is right. I like money as much as the next man, but I have discovered that pursuing it over spending a little time with something other than work has been more than profitable. An hour's solitary walk, a few minutes listening to the wind in the trees, those precious minutes of reading before I turn out the light on my day, have all been worth gold to me. Along the way have come many ideas for writing and the satisfaction that I have lived in the skin of the place I call home.

Years ago, I read an essay by a college student who had come to envy her grandmother's simpler world. The older woman had always been willing to spend countless hours making pies from scratch. At first, the young girl thought it silly when she could save precious time by buying the pie at a bakery or supermarket, then use those extra minutes for other pursuits. That is until she realized that all the time she was "saving" was either spent working or wasted on social media or watching a television program that she couldn't even recall a few minutes later.

"With a little determination," Lightman writes, "each of us can find a half hour a day to waste time. When we do so, we give ourselves a gift. It is a gift to our spirit. It is an honoring of that quiet, whispering voice. It is a liberation from the cage of the wired world…"

There is no call for meditation coming my way soon, no mail-order course to help me with this revolutionary process, no trips to a professional who will try a talking cure or help me find inner peace. But one statement that Lightman makes in his pencil-thin book is going to stay with me a while, and I thought of it again today as I lagged behind my grandson as he and his grandmother and younger brother all walked a sun-lit trail in the woods. The sky was blue, and the oaks and maples were beginning to show fall color, and not once did I check my watch or phone.

Lightman wrote that he can still easily—instantly—feel the jolt that surged through his arms at the perfect hitting of a baseball when he was a smallish, non-athletic boy of twelve. Somewhere in the recesses of his spirit, that boy and that feeling of elation still live.

"I hope that I will always have moments of quiet to feel and touch him," Lightman says of that young self and that special memory.

Henry Brooks Adams remembered a day spent fishing with his father in a similar way, and if we'll take the time, we all have special moments tugging at us, ready to be relived, just like the first time we felt the tug of a fish on the line.

Mike Lunsford

NOTHING NEW FROM THE WESTERN FRONT
November 11, 2018

I own a book called *Parke County in the World War*. Published in 1920 by The Rockville Tribune, the school yearbook-sized volume lists the names and uniformed portraits of the soldiers and sailors and Marines from my county who served in World War I. Of course, when it was released, there was no hint that another, even bigger, war was coming; even a few more after that one…

There are over 600 pictures in the book, and sadly, five pages are devoted to the 40 men—the "Gold Star Boys"—who died fighting in Belgium and France, an unusually high number I think for such a rural county as mine. One of those men—Tony Kashon—was just 23 when he was killed fighting with Battery F of the 150th Field Artillery, Rainbow Division. His gravestone is in Rosedale Cemetery, not far from my grandparents' marker.

Some of the men shown in the book ended up in uniform again in the years to come. That was, I'm sure, unthinkable to the merchants and coal miners, the housewives and schoolchildren, the farmers and brick makers living here 100 years ago when the "war to end all wars" was finally over.

By then, the world's population was some 50 million lighter after the war's carnage and Spanish Influenza had done their work.

The book is one of two copies I have and only cost a few dollars at an auction, yet it serves as a reminder to me

This Old World

that the First World War, and all the wars before and after it, no matter how often we say otherwise, can be forgotten and unappreciated, relegated to the dusty pages of history books, professorial lectures, and late-night television documentaries.

There is a great danger in that inevitability, in the disturbing trend of forgetting our own history, and thus being doomed to make the same mistakes again. *New York Times* writer, A.M. Rosenthal, suggested the same thing after he noticed that people seemed to be forgetting what happened in the death camps, so he wrote about it in "No News from Auschwitz" in 1958, a little over a dozen years after World War II ended.

I had planned to write today of something other than the centennial celebration of the first Armistice Day. The day became an official holiday in 1919 by presidential decree, but the fighting itself stopped when the artillery was silenced at the 11th hour of the 11th day of the 11th month, 1918, and the work of re-building a new world lay ahead.

Today is going to be a day of observances, a day for cemetery ceremonies and school programs, and speech making; a federal holiday. I hope it is more than just that though.

No matter how much I have read of the "Great War," I know that I can never appreciate it, not its muddy trenches or poison gas, its U-boat attacks on innocents and murderous, outdated, and nearly criminal battle tactics.

It doesn't seem possible, but I knew some of the

men who served in the war, a few of the faces in the book impossibly youthful, yet familiar. One was Dee Cottrell, who owned the local mortuary business in Rosedale for years. My family entrusted Dee to a good number of our burials, but when I saw his solemn manner and felt his hand on my shoulder at my grandfather's funeral, I had no idea that he had been "over there." The book lists him as a coal miner, as does the county draft index I stumbled upon when poking around online.

Glenn Williams, who lived to be nearly 101, was in both the book and in the draft index, and so were, I believe, dozens of men I unknowingly passed on the streets or in the grocery stores when I was a young boy. What a sobering thing it is now as a "senior citizen" to realize that those old men then were just 20 or so when they were shipped off to France, that they were all born in the 19th century, that they all had stories they could have told…

The book also matter-of-factly states that William Isham, a Parke County farmer who had a young wife, was killed on July 25, 1918, the same day that his friend, Blaine Fellenzer (a Purdue student), was also killed. The book's compiler thought it ironic that Fellenzer died fighting against a country from which his own grandfather had migrated to escape a "terrible system of oppression." It is also noted that Fellenzer's very best friend, Henry Hopper, who trained with Fellenzer and left on the same troop transport with him, was killed in action in nearly the same spot—along the Vesle River—just 13 days later.

This Old World

Ironic, to me, is that the last four men listed in the draft registry I discovered were all from Mecca and Carbon; all were "laborers" and all were from Turkey. They were just a few of the immigrants who came here to work in our small town brick and tile plants and coal mines. Virtually everyone who came from my township was listed in the registry as miners or farmers, the former outnumbering the latter four-to-one.

The book's editors included a number of poems and essays by county natives—a few by well-known journalist Juliet Strauss—and additional information about town and school activities and county-wide organizations, clubs and churches during the war, which serve as reminders how united we seemed to be during the Great War. That in itself is sobering as we observe Veterans Day today at a time when it seems we are anything but united.

There is no news—nothing trending—from the Western Front today, but whether we want to believe it or not, the terrorism, the crumbling of great empires, the rise of radical nationalism and despotism are as much with us today as they were in 1914, when the war first began.

That is, I guess, why I wanted to write about the Great War today. It shows us that we have already had tougher times than the ones we are in now, and that forgetting that, and losing touch with our own history is more than embarrassing; it will haunt us.

Mike Lunsford

A CARDINAL AT MY WINDOW
December 2, 2018

A friend wrote last week to tell me that he hadn't seen many cardinals around his yard; he wanted to know if I had noticed their absence too. Since we keep our birdfeeders full and live at the edge of the woods, I told him that we had seen and heard cardinals all fall, although more now than a month ago.

Cardinals are one of the blessings of paying attention to trees. Since I believe that the less-celebrated females, with their warm-brown chest feathers and red-orange crests and bills are one of the prettiest birds, I never fail to take their pictures. I am doubly happy to see their more colorful mates are never far away.

It is true that cardinal couples commit for "life," a term that means they live together for at least a year, or until one or the other dies. By late in the fall, they'll be singing more, not because they aim to please us at the onset of winter cold, but because they are like old husbands and wives—one mate completing a sentence before the other has finished…

Cardinals have other characteristics that are similar to humans. For instance, it is the female that actually builds the nests—usually at least two or three a season—while the male sits about and chatters.

That is somewhat like it is in my house; as I sat near my window beginning this story, Joanie was baking and boiling and basting a Thanksgiving feast, happy, no doubt, that I was out of the house and her way.

Female cardinals are not only into the home construction business, they incubate their eggs alone, although the male does dutifully feed her as she sits on the nest. After their brood is hatched, they are a dedicated and hard-working couple, seeing to it that their young are well-fed and warm. Not long after the kids are ready to leave—about two weeks after they hatch—the female begins to raise another family; she does so up to four times a year in nests that are cups of woven weed stems, twigs, and strips of bark, sometimes even grapevines.

Male cardinals, however, are hardly preening slackers. They ferociously look out for their mates and youngsters, fighting off interested suitors, sometimes mistaking their own reflections in windows for intruders. It isn't unusual to hear of someone who has a cardinal pecking away at its own image on a living room window as if he's lost his mind.

Besides the big open seed-filled tray I keep tacked to a front yard maple tree, there are places not far from my house where I am guaranteed to find cardinals. One is a thicket of tangled wild rose briars, scruffy trees, and brush a short walk below us in the woods. The leaves have nearly all dropped now, so by the next snowfall, I should be able to slide down our hillside to the spot. At first, the cardinals will scatter as I come near, but slowly they'll make their way back to bejewel the branches in a nervous crown of color; all I have to do is stand still and endure the breeze and the cold mush on which I stand.

There is, of course, as much folk legend about cardinals as just about any other bird. The Cherokee supposedly believed redbirds were a symbol of the sun and the creation of the world, and, of course, there are some who believe they bring messages from Heaven. I never fail to see someone's social media post about seeing cardinals and it being a sign that a lost loved one is staying in touch. If that is truly the case, a little magnolia tree near our front feeder becomes a family reunion of sorts come any snowfall.

One reason I love cardinals is that they stay put, living in the same areas for years if the food supply is reliable. Unlike many other birds, cardinals also seem to be expanding their range, perhaps inching farther northward as our summers grow longer and our falls and winters warmer. They are also communal, living in small bands, a few birds of the group foraging while others stand as look-outs for trouble.

They can be long-lived too; for instance, one banded female lived nearly 16 years, a remarkable fact considering they are as vulnerable to predators as the "redcoats" were to guerrilla attack by sniping colonists during the Revolution. The birds are so popular that seven eastern states (their range does not get much farther west than Nebraska and Kansas) have named them their state bird, including Indiana and Illinois.

Last week, we bundled our grandsons up and

walked a familiar trail for a mile or so. The trail ends abruptly, unable to stretch any further into a farmer's field, and so a mound of dirt has been piled up to serve as both stop sign and brush pile. The place is a tangle of wild thorns and honeysuckle and mulberry.

While Joanie tended to the younger, I pushed forward into the brush with the older, telling him to step quietly because I hoped to take pictures of the cardinals I had seen as we neared. Of course, he crashed into the place like a baby rhino, and in an instant the birds fled for their lives; I think he believed they would come to him, that they were tame. We stood for a few minutes more, and soon, we watched as the cardinals sifted back in around us, curious, but wary.

With some irony, a female cardinal landed on my cabin porch today as I sat at my keyboard, chin in hand to watch a squirrel as he scaled a sycamore tree like a skyscraper daredevil. I keep a shallow bowl of water on the railing for the birds, and she came to sit on its rim, her back to a snowy brisk wind that tousled her head feathers into a frazzled pompadour.

Within a few seconds, she was gone.

THOUGHTS OF SILVER BELLS
December 24, 2018

The gray skies and chilly northwest winds of the day I write this seem appropriate for Christmas stories, particularly since my grandsons are in our warm house a few steps away from my cabin door.

The boys are straining my wife's patience as they paw the decorations she's put out since they were last over, but it won't be long before they're storing memories of their own special Christmases, as we all have. I suppose plucking Joanie's angels and Santas and colorful magi from shelves and bookcases and window sills will be among their first remembrances.

Call it dull-headedness or poor sleep or just becoming forgetful, but I couldn't recall many tales about Christmases from long ago that I haven't told you before. That doesn't mean I don't have a story though…

We backed out of the drive one morning last week for a trip to town, our radio tuned to a holiday music channel that I normally wouldn't tolerate had it not been mid-December. The station has been playing Christmas songs since before the Halloween candy bowls were emptied, which, despite having a warm spot for holiday music, I think is pushing it.

Anyway, Bing Crosby was crooning away at "Silver Bells," and Joanie and I nearly spoke at the same time to say that it was getting to be the time of year to watch *The Lemon Drop Kid*.

We're sentimental sorts, so each year it has become tradition for us—whether we be together or at opposite ends of the house—to watch *It's a Wonderful Life* or the lesser-known Bob Hope classic.

Kid (1951), based on a story by Damon Runyon, is

about a small-time con artist named Sidney Milburn (aptly nicknamed for his ever-present box of lemon drops) who is given until Christmas to come up with $10,000 or end up in cement shoes, courtesy of thug Oxford Charlie.

Of course, Milburn attempts to raise the cash by running a scam involving phony bell-ringing Santas (primarily Gloomy Willie, played by William "Fred Mertz" Frawley) and a rest home for penniless old gals (one being Nellie Thursday, portrayed wonderfully by Jane Darwell).

In our favorite scene, the Kid and his love interest —Marilyn Maxwell's Brainey Baxter—sing a beautiful rendition of "Silver Bells," which, although written for the film by Jay Livingston and Ray Evans, was already becoming a holiday standard. Crosby and Carol Richards recorded the song for Decca Records in the fall of 1950 before the film's release, so with higher expectations for the movie version, Hope and Maxwell were brought back into the studio to re-record a more elaborate arrangement just before "Kid" was released—rather oddly, I think—in the following March.

My wife and I grew up with the Bob Hope movies and songs like "Silver Bells," and despite being rather open-minded about more recent Christmas music, we find it interesting that most contemporary artists still opt to sing the old classics. There's little doubt that the best Christmas songs were written between the years just before and after World War II. Certainly, I have never heard anyone do "White Christmas" as well as Crosby, and no one can touch

Mike Lunsford

Judy Garland's "Have Yourself a Merry Little Christmas" or Nat King Cole's "Christmas Song."

Although there is a nice Wikipedia entry on "Silver Bells," I went in search of a little more back story and found it in a book I'll undoubtedly use again: Philip Furia and Michael Lasser's *America's Songs, The Stories Behind the Songs of Broadway, Hollywood, and Tin Pan Alley* (Routledge, 2006).

I hadn't thought much about the origins of "Over the Rainbow" and "When You Wish Upon a Star," and so many other classics when I grabbed the book off a library shelf, but I soon realized it tells the stories of old songs we still hear today that have become part of our culture. I have to admit that, whatever I'm doing, I still pause to listen to the timeless voice of Cliff "Ukulele Ike" Edwards as he morphs into Jiminy Cricket; I grew up with his Disney-inspired song from Disney's "Pinocchio," even though he first sang it in 1940.

According to the book, "Silver Bells" has sold well in excess of 150 million copies, and for years, Livingston referred to it as "the annuity." At first, the songwriters resisted the assignment of writing a Christmas song, saying, "Every year everybody sings the same old Christmas songs, and the new ones never seem to make it." They had the doubly-tough task of writing a song for the film about Christmas in a big city.

Gaining inspiration from a small silver bell Evans kept on his desk, the pair wrote what they first called

"Tinkle Bells," about "the people who stand on street corners tinkling their bells." When Livingston's wife told him that the word "tinkle" had a different connotation than what he had in mind, they wisely changed the name.

By the time we made it back home, Joanie and I had heard "Silver Bells" three times, each version by a different singer, including one rendition by Rosemary Clooney and another by Brad Paisley. For us, though, there's nothing quite like the version from *The Lemon Drop Kid*.

ROD SERLING SPEAKS TO US
January 14, 2019

A sabotage-minded gremlin wrecking a rain-blasted passenger plane engine; an owlish little man crying over the shattered lenses of his eyeglasses amidst a bomb-blasted landscape; a young woman peering over her car's steering wheel at a cadaverous hitchhiker who seems to be everywhere she goes…

Those timeless images from *The Twilight Zone* kept me wide awake in the black-and-white reruns of my childhood living room; they keep me watching even now.

I think I knew, even at age 10 or 11, that the show was teaching something to me; perhaps that's why I was allowed to commandeer our boxy, tubed Philco—the lights out, a bowl of popcorn in my lap—all those years ago. Creator Rod Serling's ominous voice bookending each episode, his smoldering cigarette, his words of warning, pulled me toward the lateness of the hour. And, the series' memorable storylines made me think, something that Serling certainly felt was becoming rare.

"We're developing a new citizenry," he told a newspaper reporter. "One that will be very selective about cereals and automobiles, but won't be able to think."

A ventriloquist's dummy that not only takes over the act but his puppet master's life; a bed-ridden old woman who gets late-night phone calls from a long-dead fiancé; a man who can freeze time with a special stopwatch; an Army lieutenant who sees a pale purple light in the faces of the men he is to send into battle…

At a time when we have a seemingly unlimited and ready supply of television viewing options, *The Twilight Zone* remains available in holiday marathons, via live stream, and, for me, in the form of a gifted set of DVDs. CBS ran the series mostly on Fridays from 1959-1964, and despite praise from critics, it struggled for decent ratings, suffered inconsistent sponsorship, fought budget constraints, and sometimes created controversy.

Award-winning author, illustrator, and lecturer, Arlen Schumer, who has written *Visions from the Twilight Zone* (Chronicle Books, 176 pages), says that appreciating the show for its influence on television and pop culture is important, but heeding its messages is more critical for us right now. He says the episodes are like all great art: "It should not only address the times in which it was made, but speak to us in the future…"

Four crooks who rob a train of its bullion, sleep for a

This Old World

century, then discover that gold is worthless but greed ever-present; a tired ad executive who walks back in time to his own small-town childhood, only to realize he can't relive it; a German u-boat captain who is doomed to repeatedly experience—as a passenger—the sinking of the freighter he has torpedoed; a man who must fend off his neighbors at the door of his own bomb shelter as atomic missiles reportedly streak toward America…

The series "…eerily forecasted the times we're living in today," Schumer told me in late December. "…its memorable messages and morality lessons, its unforgettable twist-endings and great actors' immortal performances—and Rod Serling's utterly unique voice and persona, both verbal and visual—have allowed it to live on in American pop consciousness, for us to be entertained and educated, going on 60 years now."

Schumer mentions Serling's "metaphorical children" who were influenced by the show: Steven Spielberg to Steven King, George Lucas to Jordan Peele. So too, one of the great strengths is the writers of the 156 episodes: Richard *I Am Legend* Matheson, creepy Charles Beaumont, Earl Hamner, who created *The Waltons*, George Clayton Johnson, and, of course, Serling himself, who wrote nearly half of the teleplays, many adapted from both classic and contemporary stories.

Art Carney, Robert Duvall, Agnes Moorehead, Gig Young, and Lee Marvin are but a few of the top-shelf actors who starred in the mostly half-hour programs, and composer Bernard Herrmann's work on a handful of scores underlines Serling's desire for quality.

Serling's experiences in the South Pacific during World War II came to play a key role in his writing and political thinking. Referred to as the "angry young man of television," he also drew from the horrors of the nuclear age, the undercurrent of racism and discontent in American suburbia, and the McCarthy witch hunts. He died at 50, a decade after *The Twilight Zone* left the air.

Acknowledging the multiple television remakes over the years (and the Spielberg-produced '83 film), Schumer feels that no one has been able to emulate Serling for many reasons.

"They've all missed the boat at the dock by filming in color, which totally dismisses a core concept: it was a black-and-white show in concept, as well as execution. It dealt with the netherworld between reality and dream, between life and death, between the individual and The State, between time and its discontents." Remember, Serling himself says, "…the middle ground between light and shadow."

Schumer adds that imitators have never been able to maintain "an individual guiding light" and are "conceptually empty, hollow exercises in futile, flaccid storytelling." He's optimistic for Peele's CBS series-to-come later this year, saying, "Let's hope he has the pull to get it shot in black and white."

As for Schumer's favorite episode, it's one Serling

wrote: "The Eye of the Beholder." About a young woman who undergoes failed surgical procedures to fix her "horribly deformed face" because of a desire to look like everyone else, Schumer says, "It's an artistic tour-de-force, choreographed like a ballet and lit like a German Expressionist film. Its twist ending is perhaps the most unforgettable of all."

For me, it may be "The Obsolete Man," a story also written by Serling and set in an eerily-familiar future where technology and totalitarianism threaten humanity and free thought. It, like the timeless, "Time Enough at Last," features the meek, yet powerful Burgess Meredith (who did four TZ episodes) as Romney Wordsworth.

Images aside, Serling's words may mean even more to us now. Looking into the camera and speaking in his halting trademark baritone, he closed the episode, "The Shelter," with this: "No moral, no message, no prophetic tract, just a simple statement of fact: for civilization to survive, the human race has to remain civilized."

MARION JACKSON WAS A GIFT
February 25, 2019

Twenty years ago, I read a short essay by Marion Jackson. In it, he described how, as a boy of 13, he climbed to the top of a huge beech tree to retrieve the eggs of a red-shouldered hawk a neighbor had killed.

Nearly 80 feet from the ground, he hesitated long enough amid the swaying branches to button the eggs into his shirt pockets, then gazed out across the "undulating tree crowns" of the Ripley County forest below him. He wrote that the trees had "...the first wash of spring greening," and "I beheld a sight that I will never forget."

We lost Marion a few weeks ago. At 85, he had lived a life that was as rich and full as a man can have; he was a gift to us, a treasure. His memories and observations, written in the cadences and language of a poet, are with us still, but Marion's legacy also lives on through the land he worked hard to preserve and the many friends who already miss him. He wanted future generations to experience what he said was the opportunity, "...to develop a deep and abiding kinship with the landscape and all of its life."

I knew Marion, although not well enough; he kindly endorsed one of my books years ago, knowing, hopefully, how much I admired his magnificent *The Natural Heritage of Indiana* (Indiana University Press, 1997, 482 pages), a massive anthology of essays, photographs, and maps that he both edited and contributed to.

I consider it the best single volume about the natural history of the state I've ever seen, and I often find myself gravitating to its heft when writing or thinking about a bird or tree, an outcropping of stone or a patch of weeds.

Born August 19, 1933, on a 160-acre farm south of Versailles, Indiana, Marion spent his childhood in both self-sufficient work and outdoor exploration, awed by a life in tune with tilled soil, blackberry patches, and a rock quarry pond. Along with his small school, and even smaller church, that patch of earth constituted the world of Tanglewood, and, as he put it, "We grew up close to the land, and its multitude of creatures, living life in a way that enabled us to see ourselves as part of the environmental web that supports all life."

For a man who accomplished so much, Marion remained true to his roots, as he said, to the "world that was to stay with me throughout the rest of my life." From a family of nine trying to feed itself on a little corn, winter wheat, and chickens, to the U.S. Navy Reserve, to earning his doctorate at Purdue University, to a long and distinguished teaching career at Indiana State University and Saint Mary-of-the Woods College, Jackson never forgot the "horse-powered farm in southern Indiana." Despite its lack of electricity and indoor plumbing, those rural days ingrained in him a healthy fear that a totally urbanized existence leaves us bereft of the simple riches of nature.

Always educating, instructing, and teaching those virtues, Marion became deeply involved locally with, among many other organizations, the Wabash Valley Audubon Society, TREES, Inc. (along with the late Joy Sacopulos), and the Ouabache Land Conservancy.

To the Conservancy, Marion donated 15 acres of what would become known as the Jackson-Schnyder Nature Preserve. Located just west of Saint Mary-of-the-Woods campus, the property was formerly owned by Julius Schnyder, a Swiss immigrant who bought it in 1929. Marion purchased the acreage from the family and once referred to it as his "personal retreat." It has not been logged for nearly 80 years now, and he enjoyed walking the land with anyone who was willing to wander its ravines and patches of wildflowers and listen to his stories and lessons.

"You can take the boy out of the woods, but you can't take the woods out of the boy," Keith Ruble, former Superintendant of Vigo County Parks, said of his good friend. "One of the greatest gifts that Marion left us was his influence to save natural areas of Indiana. He told me that his students were good, but they did not get what 'I got growing up.' I asked him what he meant, and he said, 'You learn about nature by personally experiencing it, but my students today learn it from books.' He sure was a good friend, and I will miss him," Ruble added.

Mary Beth Eberwein, who was a student of Marion's in courses such as Ecology, Plant Taxonomy, and Wildlife Conservation, soon became a friend and colleague; she eventually spent 16 years as director of the Dobbs Park Nature Center. She says of him, "He was not only a good teacher, but an interesting one, as well. I especially enjoyed going on field trips with him since he always had good illustrations and funny stories to entertain us… I was very impressed with Marion's knowledge of trees and their uses, and I wonder if he learned some of those from his father and grandfather."

Eberwein added, "I've never been very good at finding bird nests, so I was impressed with him when he told me about the little notebooks he kept as a child, filled with notes on the nests he had found… We all have good memories of Marion."

John Whitaker, who has spent decades studying the natural world himself, was both a fellow teacher and friend of Jackson's. "Marion often talked of his family and growing up on the farm near Versailles. Very similar to me, he hunted and fished, and gathered greens, berries, nuts, and fruits," Whitaker says. "He often said that he should have been born much earlier. We talked considerably about the human population problem." But when it came to politics, Whitaker told me that Marion simply said, "Oh, hell, John. We can't do anything about it anyway."

Laura Bakken, along with husband, George, also delighted in knowing Marion. She said, "He helped us enormously when we bought our ramshackle farmhouse near the Markle Mill Dam. All the fruit trees have since died, but we will always remember the time he spent helping us prune, or turn the cherries into wine, or harvest the apples. His stories were always fascinating, and I wish he'd written more of them down."

Over the years, Marion and I had a nodding acquaintance kind of friendship. I heard him speak a few times, but never sat in one of his classes or tagged along on one of his walks. It is my loss, for whether he knew it or not, I admired his natural life, one rougher and more hardscrabble than mine, yet one I connect to each time I head to the woods.

He wrote about and spoke of the lives of creeks and

forests, of grapevines and owls, of breezy solitude and laughter-filled friendships, and in that essay he said he feared, as naturalist John Muir had, a life of "the characterless cable of conformity."

Whenever he worried about that, I believe Marion returned to the memories of his "homeplace," perhaps of those hawk eggs, which he kept for the rest of his life, and of what he called, "the barefoot days of fencerow rambling."

MY TWO CENTS ON CENTS
March 25, 2019

At a time when we're often reminded about our differences, political and otherwise, I actually think there are only two types of people: those who screech to a halt mid-step to pick up a penny, and those who keep walking. I happen to be of the first ilk.

I really don't care whether the penny is face-up or down, whether it is new or old, whether it's made of a heftier gauge of copper or one of the newest lightweights composed of nearly 98 percent zinc; I will take it, thank you…

It could be a "penny from Heaven," a "penny for my thoughts," a "bad penny" or a "pretty penny," but I'll slip it into my pocket just the same, happily taking the risk of being called a "penny pincher."

I am not a child of the Great Depression, have never known true hunger, and no longer have delusions about saving enough loose change to buy myself that nifty chrome "Spacemaster" bicycle I never got as a kid.

I simply can't walk past money in the street, or in a parking lot, or, in the case of a convenience store check-out line last week, the 35 cents I happened upon as I bagged my own toothpaste. In that case, I offered it up to the young cashier, and she told me to "Keep it. People drop change in here all the time."

There have been rumors for years—which I hope hold no truth—that we are about to rid ourselves of pennies, that we are going to soon move to a system of "rounding up."

The United States Mint reportedly lost nearly $70 million making pennies last year, although I imagine there are plenty of other wasteful places in the federal budget that make our penny-spending ways seem "penny ante." Canada withdrew its pennies from circulation a half-dozen years ago, but I'll even stoop to pick up one of those.

There are probably two reasons why I admire pennies. First, I still fondly remember the Sunday afternoons as a boy spent in the middle of our living room floor going through the change my dad accumulated over the weeks. He kept it in a gray metal box, and every so often he'd tell me to sift through it to look for wheat pennies and buffalo nickels and Mercury dimes. It was great fun, because I never knew just what I'd find.

Besides, sorting change was something to do in a one-television household. A crowning glory of achievement would come on those rare instances when I found a penny that could be placed in one of his blue cardboard collector's folders, which remain incomplete to this day.

The second reason has a more specific pecuniary quality: poverty. Being a country kid and the son of a mother who never had an income nor inclination to include comic books, candy, and the occasional bottle of root beer in her spending, I had to raise my own funds for such luxuries. Scouring the ditches for discarded pop bottles proved to be the only answer for those small monetary issues, so I did it, grubbing and sweating in the muck and itch to earn my way to sugar dependency two cents at a time. Morgan's Variety in Rosedale abetted my enterprise, exchanging the grungy bottles for pennies.

Although I couldn't have made more than a few cents a day, I also recall the days when a few of my high school buddies and I spent time pitching pennies during the lunch hour. That racket was soon ended by our principal, not because he believed it might lead us down the path to organized crime, but because he thought we should have merely found something better to do with our time. Our penny hockey games in the cafeteria seemed to at least be somewhat of a more athletic endeavor.

The word "penny" has conflicting origins. According to Jennie Cohen's "Ten Things You Didn't Know About the Penny," the term was born with the German "pfennig" and the Swedish "penning," which were used to describe any denomination of coin. The first pennies were actually made of silver and date back to the year 790.

Americans originally called pennies "one-cent pieces," a term which remains official to this day. Despite all of the design and compositional changes over the years, we must love them, for we have minted over 300 billion in our nation's history. According to Cohen, Benjamin Franklin probably designed the first truly American penny, which bore the image of a sun and sundial and the motto, "Mind Your Own Business." The reverse side shows a chain of 13 links—representing the original colonies—and yet another motto: "We Are One." Pennies were also considerably larger in those days.

On the rarest of occasions, I found an Indian head penny among my dad's change, but those were few and far between. Keeping in mind how old I am, it was not unusual at all to find Lincoln head pennies that dated back to their earliest days. Abe first appeared on the one-cent piece in 1909, released for the 100th anniversary of his birth. His was the first American coin to hold the likeness of a person, and I find it appropriate that the man who designed Lincoln's image for the penny—Victor David Brenner—emigrated to the United States from Lithuania to escape persecution. His work, endorsed by Teddy Roosevelt and modeled after a Matthew Brady photograph, is the longest-running design in the U.S. Mint's history.

A few months ago, my wife dug an old coffee can of pennies out of the closet. Her mother had saved and wrapped the coins over time, and Joanie wanted to take them to the bank. I told her that I wanted to look through them first and was rewarded for my trouble with grimy fingers and just four lonely wheat pennies; all the rest of the coins were younger than I am.

But that's not to say that the simple penny doesn't supply me with a random surprise. One day this winter, I was trudging my way up our back hillside after walking my woods. It was a gray day, one in which I had underestimated how cold it was, and I had accomplished little but to lose the feeling in my toes and fingers.

Yet, as I neared the house, and in a spot where recent rains had washed dirt down from the crest of the hill, I found a penny—an old one. I would have never seen it had I not had my head down against the wind. It was battered, dated 1948, and mud-caked, its "E Pluribus Unum" on one side, while Abe's face was scraped and scarred on the other. I saw no reason—standing amid the bare trees and fallen leaves that it should have been where it was.

I ungloved my hand and stooped in the cold to pick it up. After all, a penny saved is a penny earned.

WE NEED TO TRULY OBSERVE EARTH DAY
April 22, 2019

An interesting quirk of the calendar leaves Earth Day as my chosen subject today, and I have to admit that although I love to write about the natural world, I sat at my desk a good while late last week and chewed on poorly-made coffee, a knuckle, and an idea as to how to approach the topic yet again.

It may be coincidental, but a reader kindly suggested recently that I write too often about nature—birds, in particular. I didn't think that was possible, especially when I consider where I stood early one evening in mid-month. Out for my usual walk, I paused to watch a pair of snow white egrets sitting side-by-side in the rotting branches of a wetlands tree. The wind blew through their breeding plumage as they stared stolidly into the distance, and I felt I was seeing something special by just being in the right place at the right time, by simply being an observer.

I find the soil on which we live, and its birdsong and breezes, its woodland flowers and falling autumn leaves to be more interesting than the latest political and social media noises, although I acknowledge that most of the news is urgent and dire, yet on some occasional instances, promising and uplifting too.

People can, and do, disagree on many things, but one clear truth we had better wrap our heads around soon is the attention our planet needs; if not, all the trending headlines imaginable will become moot. That is what Earth Day is designed to do: to prod us into action, to tidy up the messes we are making in our own back yards. I am not excluding myself from the urgency of that message.

I sloshed through a marsh one recent sunny and warm day; it is a mucky and stinking place that challenges the limits of my water-tight boots. It is ticky and scratchy and filled with decay, yet it is an incredibly important place, for it acts like a sponge that filters the water and air of the things we belch and spew into our environment. Its soupiness is a testament to the resiliency of the Earth to clean itself if we will give it, and other places like it, the time. Similar are our overgrown fence rows and forests, our ditches and briar patches, yet they, and the life that prospers in them, are the first things we "clean," clear-cut, drain, mow, pave over, and spray.

I am convinced that if we truly pay attention to nature, really feel it, as a handful of sand; stick our noses into it, as in the musky green scent of creek water; and hear it, like the staccato jackhammer of a woodpecker, we would not be so near the precipice of climatic calamity. We protect the things we love, and we need to love what we're standing on, and make a few sacrifices for it. If that means a little effort at picking up our own trash instead of waiting for our neighbors to do it, or refusing an extra "disposable" grocery bag, then so be it.

Earth Day was established in 1970 by Wisconsin Congressman Gaylord Nelson, the tipping point for his decision coming after he'd witnessed the carnage of a massive California oil spill. In buttoned-down collar and dark-rimmed glasses, he urged Americans to believe in the democratic process and vote for environmental change; he even promoted the shocking idea that part of the massive military budget—mostly being spent on a war in Southeast Asia at the time—be re-dedicated toward an effort to save

This Old World

the planet.

"There is a great need for the introduction of new values in our society, where bigger is not necessarily better, where slower can be faster, and where less can be more," Nelson said.

Are his words any less true now than a half-century ago?

We don't have to be biologists to appreciate the land; we simply can't afford to be lazy any longer. A few nights ago I listened to Lorrie Heber, director of the White Violet Center for Eco-Justice at St. Mary-of-the-Woods College. She said that people often feel the issues surrounding climate change appear so big that an overwhelming hopelessness keeps us from doing anything at all. But quoting a favored meme, she also said, "It's just one plastic straw, said eight million people."

"It will take the actions of each of us, large and small, to slow climate change and its impacts on virtually everything on our Earth, our only home. Being mindful is the key," Heber says. "We have to think about our consumption and ask ourselves not only, 'Do I need this?' but also, 'What will become of it when I'm done with it?'"

As we "observe" Earth Day, maybe we can appreciate it even more if we experience the term literally, today, this week, this month, by pausing a while to soak in the green of spring, to notice that which normally goes unnoticed, to think of the world we are leaving for our children and grandchildren.

Mike Lunsford

THE MOREL OF THE STORY
May 6, 2019

I have written at least two stories over the years about mushroom hunting, but am compelled this spring to visit the subject again.

My first tale came eight years ago and was primarily about our ancient barn cat, Max, who used to follow us into the woods, that is until we had to start carrying him home. The second came four years later, just after Joanie and I had stumbled across a relatively rare, but inedible, mushroom—a *rhodontus palmatas*—as it grew in magnificent fluorescent orange near a rotting tree stump.

That find, by the way, prompted a field guide photographer to come to our woods to lie on a damp tarp to take more pictures than I thought practical, but he sure appeared to be excited the whole time he clicked away. We've never found the rare fungus again, and despite checking the spot year after year, I have discovered nothing more interesting there than a black snake coiled in the sun.

Boney old Max, by the way, never tried to hike the woods with us again, not because he died, but because he's now too arthritic and tired to climb our hillsides. He's 20 now, and stays close to our back step; after all, a two-decades-old tomcat that still lives outside has to be almost as rare a thing as that *rhodontus palmatas*.

This spring has been—according to countless social media posts, and even a few stories in our own newspaper—a bumper crop year for mushroom hunting, a

This Old World

subject on which I thought I was once an ordained expert.

When I was young and lived at my old home place, I used to find bread sacks of them, often spending April afternoons scrabbling around on my hands and knees looking under virtually every leaf and Mayapple our woods offered. I found so many that I gave them away, and was considered both generous and insane.

That all changed when I married and moved. Our woods may look like prime morel real estate, but it actually produced puny yields for years. I'm not saying we've never found a mushroom here, but certainly we've not experienced anything like what I had at home, perhaps most memorably near the apple orchard that once stood on a flat acre to our south. I actually used to find them growing in the sand there.

We eventually came to believe that climate change or acid rain or not holding our tongues just right had worked their particular evils in our woods, and we began to question whether we'd ever have a good season. But this year has been reasonably kind to us, and our faith in fungus has been somewhat restored. The same wet years that probably doomed the big white pine near our driveway, seem to have been good for the mushrooms.

I've heard more theories than I care to over the years about hunting techniques—some passed down from parents and grandparents. Of course, hunters still tend to search for them near decaying elm trees (some say oaks, others walnuts) that have shed their bark, in sunny glens of

Mike Lunsford

Mayapples or wood anemones, in damp ravines or south-facing hillsides, on disturbed ground or near burned woodpiles, or along open paths and lanes.

Any serious mushroom hunter has a favored walking stick, uses only a particular kind of bag, hunts only in the morning, or evening, or just before a rain, or just after one. Some people believe that you should pull the entire growth; others claim you should pinch them off and leave a little behind; some folks carry a knife to slice the stem to leave a decent-sized stump.

Of course, there's no explanation at all for bizarre mushroom finds. I discovered a clump of nice grays one year as they grew in the cypress mulch near a downspout at the corner of our house, and once found a trio of huge yellow sponges in a patch of nasty briars near a high-power line that ran along a fencerow and was usually sprayed with weed killer by the utility company.

Once, I nearly tripped over what proved to be about a pound behind my grandparents' house in a spot where my grandmother grew her rhubarb and threw her table scraps, but they never grew there again. A buddy of mine said he found six good-sized mushrooms growing in driveway white rock last week...

Naturalist and ecologist, Mary Beth Eberwein, who once considered a career in mycology—the study of fungi—at Indiana State University, enjoys mushroom hunting too.

"I've had several people tell me that mushrooms

don't grow," Eberwein says. "They do, given the right conditions. I've watched individual morels in my 'patch' grow from half the size of my little finger to four inches tall in a week or so. Another myth, in my opinion, is that deer eat them. I've left morels growing right by a deer path and never had them bothered. I do think deer kick them over occasionally, though," she added.

Eberwein also believes that climate change will eventually affect—or already has affected—our mushroom crops. "Climate change for Indiana will probably mean more rain, and morels grow best under moist conditions, so that should be good for mushrooming," she says. "Of course, morels don't like weather too much above 70 degrees, so if our springs start to get warmer, that wouldn't be ideal either."

Mushrooms are remarkable, even mysterious, things, and as Eberwein notes, each provides a habitat for tiny invertebrates. "You've probably noticed the black specks on the water when you soak a batch of mushrooms," she says. "These are tiny insects called springtails. Other creatures I've found in and on a morel include spiders, slugs, beetles, and centipedes."

With that tasty note in mind, I'll just say that most mushroom lovers dream of their delicacies rolled in eggs and flour, salted, and fried in butter. Me, I just enjoy the time in the woods while the hunt is on. I'm just glad Max doesn't seem to know what he's missing.

Mike Lunsford

'THE SEASONS RUN WITH SWIFT FEET'
May 12, 2019

We celebrate our mothers today, and I think we should do it whether they are living or not, for if you had, or have, a mom like I did—like the one my wife lost not long ago—there is good reason to celebrate a great gift, much bigger and better than can be hidden in wrapping paper.

My mom, Romelle, was a reader, and often, after I'd stopped by to cut a little of her grass or sit at her kitchen table, she would mention a book she was enjoying. A recurring memory I have of her is one in which she has a cup of coffee in one hand and a book in the other. She was partial to historical novels and Westerns, and I know that she not only loved the time she spent with her good friends on vacations, but that she also traveled in her mind, even as she lay in a hospital bed for seemingly endless days.

Born in the middle of the Great Depression, she grew up in West Terre Haute. Her father, a coal miner, died at just 39, and I believe his loss set her on a path of independence in both thought and action. A love of books grew in her as a means for both adventure and companionship, and she carried the passion for them with her to the very end.

Mom's favorite childhood author was Gene Stratton-Porter, and as she once confided to my sister, her favorite book of all was *A Girl of the Limberlost*, published in 1909. Set in the rugged beauty of northeastern Indiana's already-dwindling Limberlost Swamp, the book tells the

This Old World

story of a young girl named Elnora Comstock, who lives in poverty with a widowed mother.

"That book almost always came up when we talked," my sister, Lora, told me. "We would go for a drive every week—almost always with the windows down and in the evenings—and we'd talk about all sorts of things as we drove, mostly on the back roads."

Stratton-Porter knew the Limberlost intimately, living near it with her successful businessman husband and family from 1894 to 1912 in a wonderful 14-room home called "Limberlost Cabin." While there, she became one of the most popular novelists in America, and her field studies and observations in the marshes came to not only dominate her books, but her life. By the time she and her husband moved to a new home on Sylvan Lake, near Rome City, Stratton-Porter's books, strong conservation ethic, photography, and unbridled individuality had made her famous. She was most alarmed about the draining, oil exploration, and clear-cutting of the Limberlost, and began to use her popularity to apply legislative pressure to preserve the swamp.

Just a few years before Mom passed, my sister gave her a new copy of *A Girl of the Limberlost*, and she read it again, as she had as a young girl. I had never read it, but a few summers ago, as Joanie and I returned from a trip to a surprisingly cold northern Michigan, we drove south into a surprisingly hot and humid Indiana, near Rome City, where Stratton-Porter and her husband built their magnificent

"Wildflower Woods" cabin—also called "Limberlost North"—amid a beautiful forest.

Although they lived there only until 1919 (both of her homes are now Indiana State Historic Sites), it was on that property, some 75 years after Stratton-Porter died from injuries in a car accident in Los Angeles, that she was reburied, in the woods, a short distance from the house. She lived the last few years of her life in California overseeing the adaption of eight of her books into movies.

Joanie and I were the only two visitors to the house that day, and despite the heat and mosquitoes, we walked the same paths Stratton-Porter had walked, then toured the house, saw her darkroom, the typewriter she used for manuscripts, the parlor where she enjoyed music, and gazed through what she once called her "million-dollar window" to the lake beyond.

Tiffany Parker, the interpretive naturalist at "Wildflower Woods," says Stratton-Porter and her work are still relevant today "… as we continue to practice conservation and share her legacy with visitors. We tell her story to get them thinking like she did, to protect what we have while we still have it, so those who come after us can enjoy the same natural wonders as she did. We are lucky enough here to see evidence of her work to conserve the native species, and we continue to showcase her hard work so that more people will make those connections to the natural world and share them with their loved ones, much like Gene did for her fans."

The author had been dead 10 years when my mother was born, but I hear the words she wrote in her books through my mom's voice. Early in *A Girl of the Limberlost*, a character named "Bird Woman" tells Elnora, "If you are lazy, and accept your lot, you may live in it. If you are willing to work, you can write your name anywhere you choose." My mom could have easily said that.

But more important, it is Elnora's words that sound the most like my mother's: "To me," the young girl says, "it seems the only pleasure in this world worth having is the joy we derive from living for those we love, and those we can help."

In the year before her death, Stratton-Porter published *The White Flag*, and in it a character says, "The seasons run with swift feet." Looking back at the life I had when my mom was young and we walked in the woods together, I can attest to that.

THE OLD MAN WHO PLANTED A TREE
May 20, 2019

It was a good day to plant trees Thursday. My nature-loving brother-in-law had left four oak seedlings near my door one evening, and I wanted to get them—two red and two white oaks—out of their damp newspaper stoles and into the ground before it warmed up.

By most standards, I have enough trees to contend with; we have our own woods, and I've also planted dozens of trees over the years in and around my yard, and a good many have gone into the soil for the same reason those four oaks did: someone gave them to me, and I didn't want them to be wasted.

I often wonder—as I am cleaning gutters or raking leaves onto tarps or picking up after storms—if perhaps I have too many trees.

But, I don't question my green-leaved fate for long, particularly on mornings like today as I watched a pair of orioles high in one of our maples, chatting and picking among the whirligigs, in hopes of finding a few fresh ones, I suppose.

The maple's seeds aren't as tasty as the oranges I have left on fence posts for the birds, but they're what nature provides free of charge and when I am not home.

Of course, I have regretted planting a few of the trees we have. I lined up three spruce trees in my yard years ago that I wish I had either planted closer to my wood line, or had not planted at all. Their low-hanging branches regularly swat my face or scratch my arms, and the weeds grow under them, requiring contortions on my part come mowing time. But, other than thin them a little, I refuse to trim the tree's branches to mowing height; I think I'd rather cut them down than scar them in such a way.

The young oaks, now nestled in mulch, are soaking up a little sun along the edges of an area below our hillside; I have spent much time there this spring clearing it by hand. The grove, mostly cherry and hackberry and buckeye, is on about the flattest piece of land we own, and in this first full

This Old World

year of retirement, I started to clean it in late February, trimming low-hanging branches, cutting deadwood, building brush piles for the birds, and hacking away at ivies and sumac and wild grapevine. By true spring, I was hanging ten birdhouses that my friend Joe had made for me in his woodshop and stacking a little firewood as the fruits of my labor.

I don't expect to live to see those oaks grow to maturity—true climbing height. I say that not to be morbid, but because I know they will grow very slowly; one or two may die or be eaten by the deer. I can't expect something pencil-thin today to be two feet across anytime soon.

With that in mind, I do remember planting two red oaks on my place, seemingly yesterday. The first seedling my daughter brought home from an Arbor Day celebration at her school; I can't remember the origin of the second. Both are now arrow-straight and green and at least 35-feet tall, monuments to sunlight and the seamless passing of time; I have no regrets about planting either.

In these days of dire climatic warnings, we need to be planting more trees. They scrub our air and provide us with oxygen; the mere sight of them has been proven to relieve stress, and we already know they help filter our water and improve our property values and shade our houses. To me, they seem to be a connection to the natural world that we all need; a tree is an ecosystem in itself, crawling with and hosting life.

A week or so ago, my grandsons came to stay the

day. The older loves to work with his dad and grandpas, so I seized upon that initiative and the cool sunny afternoon to take him outside for chores. Together, we filled a few holes in the lawn with topsoil and moved rocks from an expanding flower bed and trimmed a bush that has overgrown its spot near our garage. We also relocated a tree; a magnolia that had been first planted by a sowing bird—the sprout now a foot tall and large enough to be seen poking its head above the ground cover.

With Daniel's help, we moved the tree—which will produce fragrant white blooms in just a year or two—to the edge of the woods where it will prosper beneath the shade of other larger trees. My grandson witnessed the life in the soil beneath the tree as we dug, and on its leaves, discovered the tiny eggs of some unknown insect. For his efforts that day, I have rewarded him with his own shovel for future projects.

Knowing that I have a few trees that need to come down over the next few years—one old cherry and a few looming walnuts, in particular—I have plans to put at least two more young trees in my yard. The first is a beech, so scrawny last summer when it was given to me it was hard to believe it was living, and a white pine that was given to me by the Master Gardeners of the Wabash Valley last month. Both are in temporary residence in a flower garden until I figure out exactly where I want them to go.

It is a Greek proverb that tells us that a society "grows great when old men plant trees whose shade they know they will never sit in." All I know is that there are few things better than planting a tree, but one of them is planting a tree with my grandson.

THE PURE MIRACLE OF D-DAY
June 3, 2019

To feel the history of the "Greatest Generation," I turn to Ernie Pyle, as I have this week. Looking over a calendar a few days ago, I realized that this column was to fall just shy of the 75th anniversary of D-Day, and I recalled that Pyle wrote a series of three columns describing the carnage he found on the beaches of Normandy just after the Allied invasion of Europe.

His words remain frightful and dreary, as all good stories of real war are. But, they are optimistic, too.

I know a few men and women who can reach back to recall June 6, 1944, and I wonder if they are more, or less, uneasy with what they see in the world today when comparing it to the one they saw at barely 20 years old.

By the time American troops faced the murderous German defenses of France at Omaha and Utah Beaches, two great invasions of Nazi strangleholds—in North Africa and Italy—had already succeeded, but at a great cost. There was a reason to be upbeat, even before D-Day, that things were not going to end well for Hitler and his forces.

The columns Pyle dispatched from Normandy came within a week and a half of the day the first wave of Allied troops hit those and three other beaches. His stories are mostly about the costs of war, not just in men and materiel, but in the futures of those who did the fighting: the lives they wouldn't have if they died, and the altered existences they were to live if they survived.

In the third column—called "A Long Thin Line of Personal Anguish"—he wrote about seeing a solder lying on the beach that he immediately assumed was dead, but was, instead, asleep, so tired that he slept where he had dropped.

In his hand, the GI held a stone from the beach, as if he had his own part of the place to take with him. Pyle also wrote of picking up a Bible he had found as he wandered, then placing it carefully back in the sand a hundred yards later, not knowing why he'd taken it in the first place. He wrote of the letters he saw, the sewing kits, the cigarettes, the bloody boots…

By living with the men who fought the war, Pyle was sensitive to who they were and what they experienced. He said war was mostly a dirty, often boring, and always a terrible business. That is the kind of thing that we need to remember this week—still in the shadow of Memorial Day—that often, sacrifice is driven by no more than a sense of obligation, a determination to pay forward freedom, not necessarily hand-off comfort or success or affluence.

My generation, and the one after it, has not gone without some disaster and discomfort and gloom. We are told that we, and our children and grandchildren, are living in an age of anxiety and uncertainty, that there seems to be

This Old World

a less clear line between good and evil, that we expect much and appreciate little.

I know we haven't had nearly as much asked of us as those who fought against the Dust Bowl's winds, the Great Depression's hunger and World War II's despotism. And so, if by reading about, and thinking of, and appreciating the anniversary of D-Day this Thursday is all we can do, we should do it, whether we like "history" or not.

In the first of that series from Normandy, Pyle wrote, "As one officer said, the only way to take a beach is to face it and keep going. It is costly at first, but it's the only way. If the men are pinned down on the beach, dug in and out of action, they might as well not be there at all. They hold up the waves behind them, and nothing is being gained."

"Our men were pinned down for a while," the officer added, "but finally they stood up and went through, and so we took that beach and accomplished our landing. We did it with every advantage on the enemy's side and every disadvantage on ours. In the light of a couple of days of retrospection, we sit and talk and call it a miracle that our men ever got on at all or were able to stay on."

What those men did at Normandy was a miracle, and I see no reason why we can't make another happen as we face our own messes now. We have to move; have to get off the beaches.

At the very least, we should appreciate a miracle

when we see one.

CHECKING ONE OFF THE BUCKET LIST
June 17, 2019

Joanie and I are inveterate homebodies, but every once in a while we pack a few bags, load our wagon, and take off for an adventure. Together, we have seen the sun rise on a Maine mountainside, and watched it go down on a Montana hilltop.

We have been in crowded symphony halls, toured the homes of great writers and poets, and have stood together on a lonely beach to hear the gentle lapping waters of a Great Lake.

Still following the leads of a decidedly low-tech road atlas, we drive narrow state highways as often as we do the faster-paced interstates and eat in mom and pop places as regularly as the big chain restaurants.

Risking choices that may appear bland to some, we are fans of both the National Park Service and any state historic site. And, as those who follow my car too closely can attest, we have been known to peel off the road at a second's notice when any historical marker appears.

My mail suggests that readers tend to like stories that come as a result of our travels, and so, in anticipation of at least two photo features that will appear in upcoming months, this column condenses where we went and what we saw on another short trip we took a few weeks ago.

In what ended as a great triangle of a drive, we first

This Old World

navigated our way through considerable road construction to northern Ohio, then after just two days there, dropped down nearly to a point where there was little of southern Pennsylvania left to see. We made the final leg toward home with hardly a stop, but not before we had traveled about 1,300 miles and had checked one key item off our collective bucket list: to see Frank Lloyd Wright's magnificent "Fallingwater," called by architect Philip Johnson, "the greatest home of the 20th Century." It will be the topic of one of those features.

Before we ever saw the waters of Bear Run tumble beneath that house, we visited the beautiful northern Ohio homes of two presidents: Rutherford B. Hayes' "Spiegel Grove" in Fremont, and James Garfield's "Lawnfield" in Mentor. The life and death of the latter, and his house—dotingly expanded by his grieving wife—and his impressive tomb in Cleveland, will be the subject of the second feature.

In between all that, I am happy to report that we traveled, slept, and ate well. We saw rock quarries, met a very friendly squirrel, helped a stranded pair with a flat tire, went well off our intended route by mistake but were rewarded with an isolated graveyard that held an American legend, thought I-90 through Cleveland at 5 p.m. surely rivaled any Grand Prix racecourse, and became convinced that Indiana's roads were the worst, Ohio's fields the wettest, and Pennsylvania's rocky hillsides and roaring creeks the prettiest.

Leaving home later than we had planned, we soon

discovered that whatever could delay us on our first day on the road, did. I didn't regret spending time to help change the flat at an Indianapolis gas station (the lug nuts had been tightened by Thor), for we weren't going anywhere quickly anyway; I-465 just then was jammed with hot, creeping, construction-delayed traffic. So, instead of the typical interstates, we crawled off the capital's northeast side and rode a surprisingly smooth and scenic Highway 36 well into Ohio, stopping only to move a wayward painted turtle whose precarious choice to cross the road near Palestine forced me to risk life and limb as I dodged cars coming from two directions.

We missed a turn as we approached Greenville, Ohio, and by chance headed north on Ohio 127, which led us through green countryside, past the incredible St. Aloysious Catholic Church near Carthogena, and a trip up a side road to Brock Cemetery, the beautiful and isolated graveyard that holds American legend Annie Oakley and her sharp-shooting husband, Frank Butler. Literally just a few feet off County Road 98, the graveyard had many more stories to tell than just Oakley's.

Born Phoebe Ann Mosey in 1860 a few miles north of where she is buried, Oakley learned to shoot a rifle to help feed her family, eventually defeated the then-legendary Butler in a match, and then married him in 1882. After years of travel with Buffalo Bill and his "Wild West Show," she returned to Ohio in 1901 and spent the rest of her days performing for and donating to local charities.

This Old World

But Brock Cemetery proved to be typical of the stops we make on our trips, both for its beautiful statuary and intriguing stories—like that of PVC Douglas Eugene Dickey, who won the Congressional Medal of Honor for bravery in Vietnam, and that of the three Rue Brothers who are buried to the west of Oakley and Butler. Two of them died in battle in World War II, while a third survived wounds to come home.

Joanie and I wandered about the cemetery, which recorded its first grave in 1803, knowing we were burning time that could have been spent getting farther up the road, but the place held us there. By the time we made it to Fremont, we felt as though we had driven farther than we actually had. Three inches of rain during that first night in northern Ohio inundated already soaked field and ditches, and we saw a number of homes sitting in water that had risen nearly to their first-floor windows.

By the time we were back, we had seen a 200-year-old covered bridge; had found the spot where British General Edward Braddock had been killed in battle and secretly buried by his men during the French and Indian War; had seen two original Diego Rivera paintings; had been near the site of the terrible Darr Mine Disaster of 1907; had spoken with a 90-year-old photographer who had resisted visiting Wright's house for years, but later told me it was one of his last great adventures; and, had driven stretches of the gorgeous Laurel Highlands Scenic Highway.

Mike Lunsford

We had passed under Twilight Hollow Road, cruised through the towns of Lover and Reagantown, glided past Glyde, and by-passed a burg called Eighty-Four. We drove through the chimney of West Virginia in a driving rainstorm, found a newly-born fawn as we walked a wooded trail, and explored the fireproof chamber that held a wreath Queen Victoria sent for President Garfield's casket.

We found exactly what we were looking for, but, as usual, got to see so much more.

SUMMER DAYS WITH CREEKS AND CRAWDADS
July 1, 2019

In the lazy hot days of my July childhood, our family occasionally visited my Great Aunt Grace at her little farm in Putnam County. Grace was a younger sister of my grandmother, and since her husband had passed, we made a point of driving over to sit in the Sunday shade of her back yard to talk a while.

Grace reminded us so much of my grandmother, who had died at 60, that it was almost unearthly to be around her; her laugh and touch, her smile, were so similar that I think she served as a great comfort to us. I still remember how tiny her house was, and I don't recall her having a television, even a fan. And so, inevitably bored with lawn chairs and adult conversation, my sister and I, and sometimes our cousin, Renee, would scuff rocks down a winding gravel drive to a railroad-tie tractor bridge and explore a branch that wandered through the farm.

This Old World

There is a natural attraction to water for country kids, which we certainly were. I spent nearly as much time in the marsh near our house, or at Spring Creek, or on a nearby pond—even in a big drainage ditch near our cousin's place—than I did in my own bedroom. My summers were about dragonflies and horsetails, lightning bugs and crawdads, the latter of which lived in abundance at Grace's.

I can still see us, face-down on the bridge, dangling a bit of string between the ties, hoping to catch one of the great green-brown crawdads that we spied in the water or along the spongy banks. Half afraid of what we'd do when we actually landed one, the crawdads most often let loose and plopped back into the water before we got them an inch or two above it.

Crawdads (also known as crayfish and crawfish) are remarkable things; freshwater relatives of lobsters, there are hundreds of species; 99 percent are native to North America. Most of what I came across when I was a kid were undoubtedly burrowing crawdads, known for building "chimneys" of mud. The soil for those mounds is pushed out of vertical shafts that can run as deep as 15 feet, for crawdads keep burrowing until they've reached the water table.

I would imagine that there is hardly anyone who has spent much time outdoors who has never seen a crawdad chimney, and since they are known to prefer poorly drained soils—often heavy with clay—the accumulated weight of the dirt they dislocate on a single acre has been estimated to total over a ton, that statistic according to James Nardi in his wonderful, *Life in the Soil* (University of Chicago Press, 2007).

The most likely chimney-building burrowing crawdad in Indiana—there are five species—is the "digger" crayfish (*Fallicambarus fodiens*). Early this spring, I found a digger—I think—as I walked in the wet gravel of a field road near my house. It appeared to be perfectly at home in either the muddy brown water of a tractor tire rut, or scrabbling among the rocks, but in either place, it didn't particularly want me around.

Spending time with crawdads, as I used to, certainly made me immune to any temptation of ever eating one. As great a delicacy as they may be around the world—particularly in Louisiana—I think I'd rather eat one of my gym socks than something that smells and looks like our ditch-loving friends. It is my understanding that, like lobsters, the tail of a crawfish is what is most edible, which is no comfort to me either. Crawdads, by the way, feed on a wide variety of both living and dead plants and animals, and often their speed belies the images we have of them as lumbering and awkward. In fact, small crawfish can move with amazing speed, particularly when in reverse.

Carissa Lovett, naturalist at the Dobbs Park Nature Center—one of my grandsons' favorite places to visit—says much more study could be done on crawdads. Carissa's stories remind me that children of all ages have surely spent some time with a crawdad or two.

"As kids, we would try to catch them in the creek," Lovett says. "I even kept a couple of small ones as 'pets,' but if I remember right, they didn't make it very long."

Carissa informed me that Indiana actually has a crawdad named for it: (*Orconectes indianensis*), first described by William Hays in 1896; he classified it with another species, but they were given separate status a few years later. The Indiana Crayfish lives almost exclusively in southwestern Indiana, and other than the same threats all crawdads face (loss of habitat and invasive species) they seem to be doing just fine.

The rather featureless rusty crayfish—also native to Indiana—is labeled an invasive in many places. Bait retailers have marketed it to a point where at least five other states to our north and west fear their native crawdad populations may be threatened by these aggressive newcomers.

Although crawdads are interesting, it is the childhood connection that most intrigues me. Lovett said, "I remember lifting big flat rocks slowly and letting the water settle to see what was hiding beneath. Most of the time there was nothing, but we did get a prize under some of the rocks: crawdads, salamanders, small fish, and sometimes a small snake would surprise us. Those days spent in the woods increased my love for all things wild and is one of the factors that made me the naturalist I am today."

Good things happen to those who play in creeks.

Mike Lunsford

WE NEED ANOTHER AMERICAN MOONSHOT
July 15, 2019

As we do each year, my family slouched in lawn chairs at a 4th of July celebration and gawked at fireworks as they burst against a humid summer sky. The requisite live music had blared its way to an end only moments before dark, and the scent of popcorn and smoke from children's sparklers hung in the air like old memories.

Although a breeze had picked up and it was cooling a bit after a long hot day, my thoughts turned to the moon—just a slim waxing crescent—that never showed itself, tucked behind clouds that promised more rain by morning.

Dozens of past Independence Day remembrances have undoubtedly run together for most of us, but I doubt few of our generation have forgotten the night we watched Neil Armstrong step onto the lunar surface; it was 50 years ago this Saturday.

Like millions of other families, ours circled the television set and watched and listened in rapt attention at fuzzy black and white images and garbled transmissions between Mission Control and Apollo 11's crew for hours. Included among the scenes was the critical split that Eagle made from Columbia before its descent; then the edgy touchdown it made in The Sea of Tranquility; and then Armstrong clambering down a narrow ladder to leave a footprint for the ages in the gray dust. All the while, Walter Cronkite's baritone commentary gave us a sense that absolutely nothing could go wrong, although, of course, it could have.

I believe we need a national goal—a worldwide goal—similar to the one accomplished in the days of what historian Douglas Brinkley has called the *American Moonshot*, which also happens to be the name of his current bestselling book. It may be hard to believe, but even in their envy and fear of our technological power, many in the Soviet Union, and even more around the world, were rooting for Michael Collins, Buzz Aldrin, and Armstrong as they took their flight toward making that "giant leap for mankind."

There are plenty of alarms ringing in the news that suggest American ingenuity is dying, that we are being passed by as we languish in a consumptive idle, that "Made in the USA" means less than it used to, that our work ethic has slipped. One of the most convincing pieces is already 5 years old: Michael Hanlon's "What Happened to Innovation," published in *Aeon* in December 2014.

He wrote: "…there once was an age when speculation matched reality. It spluttered to a halt more than 40 years ago. Most of what has happened since has been merely incremental improvements upon what came before. That true age of innovation—I'll call it the Golden Quarter—ran from approximately 1945 to 1971."

I don't totally agree with those sentiments, but I have to admit that I have bought some of it, particularly as I wait for the next "service representative," or stand in line to return something shoddily made, or read yet another explanation as to why I am paying more and getting less.

Are we, however, just one great goal away from regaining our technological and competitive edge, if, indeed, we ever gave it up? Brinkley's book — all 526 pages of it — is subtitled, *John F. Kennedy and the Great Space Race.* I have yet to finish, but had I stopped reading just after the author's impressive preface, I couldn't have been inspired much more.

Most of what Brinkley writes in those first 10 pages is dedicated to Kennedy's crucial vision for putting a man into space, and, even though he never lived to see it, a man on the moon. JFK's romantic sense of adventure and natural buoyancy gave us good reason in those days—despite an astronomical cost in today's dollars of over $180 billion—to want to strive to reach out to the moon. Without big ideas we stagnate, stand still; he understood that, and set the tone for a new era in this country—in education, in science, and in confidence—as he spoke at Rice University about a year before he was slain in Dallas.

"We set sail on this new sea because there is new knowledge to be gained, and new rights to be won, and they must be won and used for the progress of all people," he said.

Today, despite lessons of the past—specifically, all the good that was gleaned through our space program—we are reticent to spend money to explore the cosmos, indeed to even agree that our blue marble of a planet itself needs dire attention. Our investment in the frontiers of space has been returned times over, not only in the convenient and everyday technology we hold in our hands or watch on big screens, but in life-saving medical imagery and weather forecasting, and much, much more. As promised, the Mercury-Gemini-Apollo programs have "been used for the progress of all people."

For me to suggest that Kennedy was no "Cold Warrior," that he didn't understand the military necessity of gaining superiority in space over the Soviets, would be naïve. He knew what was at stake, but not long before he died, he also spoke of finding a ceiling for the development of military hardware for the sake of our children.

"What kind of a peace do we seek?" he asked in a commencement address at American University in June 1963. "Not a Pax Americana enforced on the world by American weapons of war. Not the peace of the grave or the security of the slave. I am talking about genuine peace, the kind of peace that makes life on earth worth living, the kind that enables men and nations to grow and to hope and build a better life for their children—not merely peace for Americans but peace for all men and women—not merely peace in our time but peace for all time."

The 4th of July has come and gone—our 243rd year of independence—and we have a long list of "moonshots" from which we can choose. Real leadership, tinged with eloquence and idealism, is important; it paves the way for big things to come.

Mike Lunsford

THE MUSIC OF THE STREAM
July 21, 2019

There has been so much written and said about Frank Lloyd Wright's Fallingwater, that I risk repeating often-told stories about both the man and the house. But, they are good stories…

My wife and I spent a warm June day in the rocky southern Pennsylvania forest visiting the spirit of the idiosyncratic architect, whose creation here springs from a hillside as a series of "reinforced concrete trays" over the rolling cascades of Bear Run Creek. We had a hard time leaving it behind to head home.

Wright built the house for respected Pittsburgh merchant and civic leader, Edgar Kaufmann. Spending nearly a year nursing his ideas, the architect, using mostly local labor and sandstone, started construction in April 1936, and by December of the next year the Kaufmanns were moving in; acclaim for the house was immediate.

By then, nearing 70, Wright's design re-ignited an ebbing career that was to last another two decades, but more importantly, it served as proof that his core belief in "organic architecture" was not merely a catchphrase. The late Philip Johnson—a great rival of Wright's—called Fallingwater, "the greatest house of the 20th century."

Kaufmann purchased the land on which Fallingwater was built—about 70 miles southeast of Pittsburgh—as a personal refuge from the noises and smells of the big city, and for years encouraged his employees to

This Old World

use the property as a vacation spot. By 1921, he and his family were spending weekends there in a rustic prefabricated "cottage" they called "The Hang Over." It had no running water, plumbing, or electricity.

First meeting the architect on a visit to Wright's home and studio (Taliesin) near Spring Green, Wisconsin, where their son, Edgar jr. (he preferred the lower case in his name), had served as an apprentice, Kaufmann, and his wife, Liliane, had both the means and aesthetic interest in hiring the eccentric Wright to build a "retreat" for them.

Ironically, it was the younger Kaufmann who first used the language so often associated with what would become Fallingwater. In reference to natural architectural design, he said Wright's concepts "…flowed into my mind like the first trickle of irrigation in a desert land."

Most of the tales about the house and the often-contentious relationship between Wright and the elder Kaufmann—who more than held his own with the bossy architect—are true. Wright invested considerable time in contemplating the design, but actually spent only a few hours hurriedly drafting the four levels of the house on a single summer day in 1935 as Kaufmann drove from Milwaukee to Taliesin. "Come right along, E.J.," Wright supposedly told him on the telephone before he began to work. "We're ready for you."

Kaufmann first believed he was reviewing months of Wright's labor, but was kept busy in a leisurely lunch and with small talk while apprentices touched up the just-finished drawings. Yet, Wright was not creating on the spur of the moment; all of his hours of envisioning the project were realized as he maintained a running dialogue with those who watched him feverishly work at the drafting table. Apprentice Edward Tafel later said, "The design just poured out of him."

Wright and Kaufmann—who maintained their friendship until the latter died in 1955—entered into many projects, mostly civic and mostly unrealized. Yet they argued about the amount of structural and reinforcing steel that Fallingwater needed to anchor and support its extended cantilevered terraces; Kaufman wanted more, and Wright less. Kaufman won out, and had he not, it is probable that the house would have crumbled into Bear Run.

In reply to a hasty note that Wright dashed off after discovering changes to his plans, Kaufmann mimicked the architect's tone, writing, "I have put so much confidence and enthusiasm behind this whole project in my limited way, to help the fulfillment of your effort that if I do not have your confidence in the matter—to hell with the whole thing."

It is also true that Kaufman believed that Wright would design the home to sit below the gorgeous falls so that those inside could look upstream toward the rolling water. Instead, Wright told Kaufman, "I want you to live with your waterfall, not just look at it."

And so, Wright planned for the terraces to extend out over the stream, similar to the branches of a tree or the

This Old World

shelves of stone that Bear Run had carved over the ages. Ironically, little of the falls can actually be seen by those in the house; the architect felt that if it were clearly visible all the time, it would soon become unappreciated. But, the Kaufmanns did, indeed, "live with their waterfall," and its flowing poetry can be heard in every room of the house.

Despite enormous financial success and a keen intellect, Kaufmann was somewhat insecure about being considered by some as simply rich. He enjoyed Bear Run and his crude cabin and originally told Wright that he would spend no more than $20,000 on the new weekend house, still quite an investment considering that the country was in the midst of the Great Depression. Instead, after seeing what Wright had in mind, Kaufman told him, "Don't change a thing."

The construction eventually cost no less than $155,000—nearly $3 million in today's dollars—and, of course, like most Wright designs, has continued to present expensive maintenance challenges. It was reported that the Kaufmanns experienced some 50 leaks in the years they occupied the house and that Liliane often complained about a lack of closet space and curtains.

All other stories aside, the time we spent at Fallingwater was magical, and a crowded parking lot and visitors' center belied its feeling of solitude and serenity. The short walk to the house down a sloping shaded ramp and graveled path is analogous to Wright's fabled narrow stairways and halls, and it reveals, first the roar of Bear

Run's waters, then the buff and glass and Cherokee red of the house; it was as if we were slowly opening a gift.

Strict, to keep unwanted hands off Fallingwater's treasures, our tour guide reminded those in our small group to avoid leaning against, sitting on, or touching anything. My camera, its lens capped while inside the house, had to be kept centered around my neck to keep it from banging into furniture or woodwork. The ceilings, typically low, actually had me instinctively stooping in several doorways, yet the more utilitarian areas of the house serve as mere passageways into great open spaces, flooded with natural light and the cadences of moving water.

Unlike most other Wright designs, the majority of the items in Fallingwater—including furniture—are original. Among them a pair of Diego Rivera paintings (the Kaufmanns knew the artist and his wife, Freda Kahlo), a Japanese woodcut that Wright had gifted to his friends for Christmas in 1937, and, of course, chairs, desks, and lamps of Wright's own design. The Kaufmanns maintained a keen passion for the arts, and the house is a trove of wonders, yet at least one virtue is not an artifact at all like their vases and sculptures.

In his earliest reveries about Fallingwater's design (the architect chose the name himself), Wright decided to employ the very boulder on which the Kaufmanns often sat above the falls: "The rock on which E.J. sits will be the hearth, coming right out of the floor, the fire burning just behind it," he said.

This Old World

Perhaps my favorite room in the house—planned as a sun-filled nook of a study for Edgar jr—serves, along with its adjoining outside stairway entrance and narrow shaded terrace, as most of the top floor; it helps to counterbalance Wright's design. From there, we crossed a sky-lit "bridge," a slim but airy walkway that leads to a small three-room guesthouse located above the main home, nearly at the crest of the hill. A 30-foot-long spring-fed pool sits slightly above that house, and it is from there—still well within hearing range of the soothing stream—that we saw native outcroppings of rhododendrons and laurel working toward late-spring bloom as water dripped from crevices in the stone.

Edgar jr. eventually entrusted Fallingwater to the non-profit Western Pennsylvania Conservancy in 1963; he continued to visit even as tours of the house were beginning, and died in 1989. With great foresight, he realized most that Fallingwater needed to be a gift, for he shared with his parents a firm belief that good design and tasteful art were public virtues. His partner, architect Paul Mayen, designed the beautiful visitor's center in 1981.

A description of the house may be summed up best by the Conservancy itself, which notes that it is "…more than the sum of its parts: the architect, the client, the architecture, the art, the land, and the period."

That is true, but even more, I like Wright biographer Merle Secrest's thoughts: "…he, no doubt, was also thinking of the background splash of water, the rustle of wind moving through the boughs, the shifting patterns of dappled light and shade, the feeling of being deep in a cave, sheltered by low ceilings and overhanging eaves, and the sense of rocks behind, as one sat beside a vast and friendly fire…"

THE SHARED EXPERIENCES OF SUNSETS
July 29, 2019

On the last evening of our yearly stay on Lake Michigan, Joanie and I—by some stroke of luck—found ourselves alone at the bottom of a very long hill of sand. Monarch butterflies were still flitting between milkweed and locust scrub and beach peas, and the air was cooling as a soft breeze came at us from the north.

We were there to watch the sun—a glowing ember of red and orange—slip below the horizon, and the scene was to serve as a glorious goodbye to the warm blue day we had spent with sand between our toes, good books in our laps, and the laughter of our grandsons in our ears. Unlike the cold front-fed roar we had heard the day before, the great lake's mood had changed, and its gentle wash now came to us in a solemn and relaxing rhythm.

Well above our spot, the noise of street traffic was steady, and dozens—perhaps hundreds—of people sat in lawn chairs, leaned on trees, and knelt in the grass, talking, adjusting cameras, and spreading blankets. Still, we felt isolated on the beach, quiet in our own thoughts, knowing we were watching another day of our lives together blink out in a not-too sad sort of way.

It is an odd thing, but without fanfare or social media post or public pronouncement of any kind, people are drawn to that particular hillside as darkness begins to creep into the skies. The ridge above the beach begins to fill by eight or so on summer evenings, and I have sat on a bench under a favored maple to watch them come by car—many never leaving their bucket seats and heaters—from the town's vacation homes and restaurants and pleasure boats, while others arrive by bicycle or on foot. There is a mixture of first-time visitors and year-round residents, kids and old coots, the affluent and those decidedly not, some in jackets and others in brimmed hats, some barefooted or still wearing swimsuits from their days in and around the lake's wonderful blue-green water.

By nine, the real show begins, particularly if there is a scud of clouds to the west. Their primary function, it seems, is to bend and fracture and scatter the waning rays of dying light. And, then, of course, the lake itself works its magic in reflecting and mirroring—nearly projecting—an impressionistic and temporary canvas for the gawkers who had to invest only a little effort and a few minutes of their time as the price of admission.

There is a shared experience in watching sunsets in such a way. On that night, Joanie sat near a wind-beaten willow in a light jacket as I paced a bit in the damp sand with my camera. There was a chill in the air and the sun was turning the beach sand to gold. I actually shivered and rubbed my bare arms; ironic, for just a few days before, it had been so hot and humid that the horizon was blanketed with a steamy superheated fog that rendered the water library quiet.

Like most long-married couples, we carried on a disjointed and nearly-whispered conversation, speaking of the events of the day, which had been like most other days for us on the lake. We talked about how we'd watched our children—and now, grandchildren—grow with each trip, and of other places we'd gone over the years. And, after we saw the very last of the sun slip below the far edges of the lake, we practically moaned at the same time as to how tired we were, and if we should have stayed at the top of the hill instead of leaving ourselves the steep walk up it.

If we are fortunate, there will be many, many more trips to the lake together, and most of the evenings there will be shared with our family, as it was with my daughter and grandson, Joe, just the night before. But, on some nights, it is just me, alone with my thoughts, which is a clichéd term, for, like so many others mesmerized by the spectacle, I usually think of nothing in particular except that there must be more to the beauty of it than mere science.

Experts tell us that watching sunsets is good for us. A few years ago I wrote a feature about the habit after reading a piece in *Psychology Today* by health writer Linda Wasmer Andrews. She said sunsets "enrich our lives" and, perhaps more importantly in these times, they give us, at least temporarily, satisfaction with what we have and who we share it with.

I'm not sure that I agree with her when she noted that appreciation of nature is a basic instinct that we all have, that it isn't learned. I would like to think that is true, but I've seen too much trash and carelessness in beautiful places to suspect it is. Yet, on that night together, Joanie and I agreed that there was a near reverence in sharing the sunset with so many others, people who were strangers, who may be at different ends of the political spectrum, yet we were there together for a few minutes to witness one true and great thing.

Andrews added in her story that watching a nice sunset "gives us a break from the worries we have, particularly those little nagging things that seem to take up space in an already-crowded mind."

I couldn't agree more, for just a while later, I closed a book, turned out the light, rolled over, and was soon asleep.

WET SPRING BRINGS SWALLOWTAIL SUMMER
August 12, 2019

As far as the calendar goes, summer runs into late September, but once the page on August is turned, I tend to believe the season is mostly gone; it's the way teachers—even retired ones—see the world.

One thing, however, is certain about this still-reasonably-young summer: it has been a good one for swallowtail butterflies, at least on my place and in my garden.

The cone flower and tiger lilies and phlox that I transplanted around my yard so many years ago enjoyed the wet spring and have been alive with hosts of those colorful friends in recent weeks.

According to my worn and wrinkled *Kaufman Field Guide*, swallowtails are among our largest butterflies. All species in the Midwest have "tails" on their hindwings, and when very young, their larvae may appear to be bird droppings, so many survive an onslaught of hungry birds, at least for a while.

What I find most intriguing about swallowtails is that each of the species seems to have a favored food source. The Eastern Tiger often consumes cottonwood and tulip poplar leaves (perhaps a reason I have seen so many of them near my cabin, for a poplar gives me shade all morning).

Zebra swallowtails, not as numerous on my property in the past, but having a great summer here now, feed on paw paws, of which I have many just below my yard on a wooded hillside. I hardly notice those trees until the fall when their huge leaves turn a pleasant yellow.

Black swallowtails feed on parsley, dill, and Queen Anne's Lace (I have plenty of the latter here too), while Spicebush swallows choose, of course, spicebush, but they like the taste of sassafras just as well. I have seen many of those this summer, and, perhaps a bit unusual for us, even a few Giant swallowtails. They prefer hoptree and rue, neither of which I could identify if it were next to me.

Jill Staake, a contributing writer for *Birds & Blooms* magazine, loves swallowtails too, and although she says it is speculation, this season may be a banner butterfly year for several reasons.

"Most swallowtails, though not all, overwinter in their pupal state—in chrysalis—emerging in spring to feed and mate. In your area, most would likely start to emerge in May, although I think you had a cooler, wetter spring than normal, so some delay could have caused more of them to wait and emerge at once, making you more likely to see larger numbers," she said from her home in Florida.

Staake also says that swallowtails have several unique features that make them stand out among butterflies: "Their caterpillars have a special organ called the osmeterium. This is a fleshy forked gland that emerges from the front of their heads above the eyes when they are startled or need to defend themselves. Their bodies use the oils from the foods they eat to coat the osmeterium in a very strong foul-smelling liquid that is poisonous, or at least repellent, to most predators."

And, although swallowtails are known, of course, for their beautiful tails, Staake says that they too are part of their defense systems.

"A predator will aim for the tails, but often end up with a mouth of useless scales, while the butterfly escapes with just a bit of wing damage. It's pretty common to see swallowtails with one or both of their tails missing, while the butterfly itself is doing just fine."

Of course, there are many misconceptions about butterflies, such as having an abundance of flowers is the only way to attract them, or that so-called "butterfly houses" work. Those structures "usually just wind up as homes for wasps and other pests," she says.

"Each butterfly species has a specific plant or group of plants that their caterpillars can eat. Having these in your yard will encourage butterflies to linger and lay eggs, rewarding you with caterpillars, and then the next generation of butterflies. And, butterflies require shelter. Rock piles, trees, ornamental grasses, and dense shrubbery can all provide protection against bad weather and predators. They also need to obtain salts and minerals, which they often do by 'puddling' on mud or wet sand. In the morning, and on cooler days, they need places to spread their wings and warm up. A large flat rock in the sun is ideal for this behavior," she adds.

One of the earliest memories I have is of butterflies. I couldn't have been more than five or six when I discovered the rather goofy-looking caterpillar of an Eastern Tiger swallowtail as I walked from my back step to my grandparents' place next door. Theirs was a long driveway of crushed coal cinders that ran up the hill past our house and near a copse of marshy woods.

On a leaf, as plain as day, inched a clownish, nearly walrus-like green worm, and I scooped it up in my hands and speed-walked it to our kitchen, holding it like a live grenade. My mom simply told me to put it back where I found it, that it "knew what to do with itself."

A few hot breezy evenings ago, I sat at my desk, and out of the corner of my eye, I noticed what appeared to be a few yellow leaves floating into the yard from the woods. I suspected that our black walnuts were shedding in what has now become a very dry month, but I soon realized the leaves were actually butterflies.

They were all Tiger swallowtails, silently gliding in from the trees to a patch of cone flowers I have kept watered near my porch rail. That moment made it worth the trouble.

SPIDER WEBS OUR "CONTINENTS OF LIGHT"
September 23, 2019

Folklore has it that seeing a spider web in the morning brings good luck for the rest of the day. If that's truly the case, I am the luckiest man I know, for a short walk to my cabin each morning has had me sidestepping and ducking them for weeks.

At the northwest corner of my little place, between the deck rail and a hanging basket of geraniums, a Hentz's Orbweaver—not a big spider at all—has been spinning, then deconstructing, her web for the past two months. She is not unlike a housewife who hangs her wash on a line in the morning, only to take it down by afternoon. Typical of her species, the spider is up early—each of her eight, dare I say, hands—tirelessly pulling back the work she started the late afternoon before. At night, and into the sunny mornings, she sits in the web's center, waiting for the pay-off.

More than once, I absentmindedly plowed through the web as I headed to the garden or walked to a bird feeder. Once, to my great displeasure, she scurried across the wreckage onto my chest and shoulder before disappearing into the safety of the plant.

That very instance is a good reason why I wear a hat into the woods this time of year, for it is inevitable that I'll wander into a web that has been strung between limbs and tall weeds, and always at about the height of my face.

In those instances, I am happy to be alone, for the unpleasant surprise often leads to a decidedly awkward dervish, with much wiping and spitting and squinting.

In the mornings, I've seen webs draped across power lines, hanging from branches high in the trees, and seen the gossamer funnels of grass spiders, wet with dew, sitting in my yard like small tornadoes. Some old-timers have touted that an abundance of webs in late summer and early fall are signs of a tough winter to come; the *Old Farmer's Almanac* is already calling for that this year, and since we are overdue for a brutal one, I think it may prove true no matter who is doing the prognosticating.

Purdue University entomologist, Timothy Gibb, doesn't buy any folklore connection to spiders, but finds arachnoids and their webs fascinating. "We find more wannabe weather predictors using the colors of wooly bear caterpillars than spider webs," Gibb says. "In either case, I

This Old World

don't put much stock into them other than to say, if you see a wooly bear or a spider web, we will likely have a winter."

According to Gibb, web-making spiders come in all shapes, sizes, and colors. Some appear to us to be "large enough to capture big birds, medium-size mammals, and even small children, while others are very tiny, as small as 1/20th of an inch in length."

He adds: "Each group of spiders has a unique life history and behavior, and of the most unusual and colorful spiders, common in yards near homes at this time of year, are the orb-weaving spiders. Orb-weavers, often called garden spiders, weave an elaborate web to ensnare their prey. Such webs are perfect displays of biological architecture."

Spider silk has been held in fascination for ages. It is remarkable stuff. Five times stronger in the same weight as steel, it can stretch up to four times in length without breaking, and is two to three times tougher than the fibers that make up "kevlar." Scientists toil at trying to synthesize artificial spider silk for all sorts of medical and engineering applications.

Gibb says, "Spider webbing (silk) is one of the most amazing materials known to man. Different silks are made for different spider purposes, but in general they all begin as a liquid composed primarily of proteins produced in the silk glands within the spider's abdomen. The liquid silk is drawn out of the spinnerets at the rear end of the abdomen and then hardens to form the silken thread upon which the web is formed. This process then allows for small liquid globules to be strategically placed by the spider in the web. These droplets are not stretched into strands, thus remaining liquid and therefore sticky. The hardened webbing, together with the sticky droplets, is what catches the insect prey and are also what elicits the web-face dance in humans."

The spider I see near my cabin is not terribly shy. If I approach slowly, she (males are rarely at home) will sit still, keep knitting, or perhaps, rappel herself down a hastily spent line a safe distance from my reach. Like others of her ilk, she has a faint cross pattern in mid-abdomen, thus her scientific name, *Neoscona crucifera*, the cross-bearer.

What may most fascinate me—besides her web-making skills—yet give me the shivers at the same time, is her ability to produce offspring. A female orb-weaving spider usually lays about a thousand eggs, hides them in a nest (probably in my plant), and by spring, when they hatch, they are wind-blown to various places and on their own to survive.

Years ago, I read Walt Whitman's "A Noiseless, Patient Spider." In it, the poet is fascinated by the quiet mark left on the world by the spinning of a single web, something we should all consider when spraying poisons or knocking a spider aside. But, more recently, I encountered Emily Dickinson, and she wrote about a spider's "continent of light," which dangled from a housewife's broom.

Spiders may create the inconvenience of webs spun in our doorways or startle us as we flip a switch in a darkened room, but their "continents of light" are among the natural world's most wondrous gifts to us.

BECAUSE WE ARE PRONE TO FORGET
October 7, 2019

In his elegiac and, perhaps, last book, *Horizon*, adventurer, environmentalist, and writer Barry Lopez includes a chapter simply called, "Talismans."

"Over the years," he writes, "I've carried home a handful of mementos, each taken from a moment or an event that might seem innocuous at the time to someone else looking on. A dozen or so of these sit atop a tall Japanese tansu [storage cabinet] in my home. I've arranged them to make intuitive sense together, the way you might arrange scenes in a short story. In this matrix they suggest to me some deeper truth about life, one that always lies just beyond my reach."

Although I have not traveled the world, nor won a National Book Award, nor written so eloquently, so passionately, about the human condition—and its uncertain future—as Lopez has, I too have collected talismans from journeys and walks and adventures. Those expeditions, tame by comparison, have been no less significant for me.

According to my yellowed dictionary, the word 'talisman' was first used in 1638 and means, "an object held to act as a charm to avert evil and bring good fortune."

But I probably use the word—and I think Lopez does, too—for its secondary definition: "something producing apparently magical or miraculous effects."

I don't mean that I keep good luck charms—a rabbit's foot or four-leafed clover—in my pocket, but rather surround myself, as Lopez does, with objects that I connect to, particularly things that I can touch or look upon to regain a sense of what I felt the day I first saw them or rolled them over in the palm of my hand. Unlike Lopez, I have no real arrangement for these things, no timeline or order to them at all, and I have considerably more than a "handful," as well.

Some may think I simply own an expanding assortment of useless junk that serves little purpose but to burden my children after I am dust, but most of my talismans are of the natural sort. If garage sales and auctions don't appeal to my progeny, then they can merely toss the things back on the creek bank or wind-blown woods from which they came.

Whereas Lopez writes of a piece of green schist he picked up in western Australia, or the cardita shells he discovered on a South Pacific island, or the 7.62mm NATO cartridge casing he pocketed in the Falkland Islands, or the 17th-century eight-real silver coin from Mexico, I have kept things that, perhaps, only a wandering boy might find valuable enough to stash in a cigar box of keepsakes. That is, if the term "boy" can also include old men who still love the crunch of a sand bar under their feet.

On my cabin shelves; on a desktop in what was once an old breezeway; in an antique tool box my dad pulled from a trash heap years ago; and, along the top of my great-

This Old World

grandmother's ancient chestnut pie safe, sits an assortment of shells, hawk feathers, bird nests, and fossils. Most of these things hold memories that now run together, yet others still take me back to exact places and times, like the egg-shaped chunk of granite on my porch rail that transports me to a sunny but cool day I spent poking along a roaring Vermont river. It may have been the Black, or could have been the Hoosic, but I recall being happy in the fresh pine air, glad I had taken the time to park the car for a stretch of the legs.

Some of my talismans constitute collections. I have blue-green Mason jars filled with buckeyes and smooth Lake Michigan stones. I have pressed leaves, and turtle shells, and deer antlers, all found on walks and rambles, most often alone, but sometimes in the good company of a patient wife or nature-loving daughter or question-filled son.

Along a window sill, near my writing desk, I keep a pile of small horn snail shells that takes me to a day I chugged up the Wabash with my brother. There also is an arrow head I found in the sand of my home place a half-century before, and a 1904 Indian head penny we discovered just this summer in the mud as it clung to a rock I brought home from my father-in-law's farm.

A few weeks ago, I took my oldest grandson for a day of adventures that ended with us walking along the creek in the late afternoon sun. I came home with a pocket of small stones and a bit of driftwood, remembrances of a day we waded together, one on which we saw an eagle, inspected the tracks of bobcats and coyotes, and saw overgrown green dragonflies hitting the water in still places.

Just before we left, we stooped to salvage a bit of glass that had been rock-tumbled to a milky green, and he saw a bone lying among some driftwood and leaves. Like the glass, its edges had been ground smooth and it looked older than it was. Although I told him it probably came from a deer, he was convinced it was prehistoric, a remnant of a once ferocious raptor. He eagerly held it as we bounced our way home in my truck, and it now resides on a shelf in his room.

Before Lopez is done pondering his talismans, he writes: "These mementos of travel sit apart from one another on the tansu. The generous space I've left around each is meant to leave each room for its aura. As I pass them by, year after year, going back and forth to a room where I work, each object remains piquant for me, eloquent in its silence. The staggering diversity of life, the stony flesh of the ancient planet, the lethal violence of human behavior, the growing inutility of war in the modern era… I glance at them because I know I am prone to forget."

My talismans are less organized, less dramatic. But we keep these things for the same reasons.

NATURE'S CUSTODIAL ENGINEERS
October 21, 2019

Surely, one of the homeliest animals known to man

This Old World

is the turkey vulture. With its horror-mask countenance and Bela Lugosi-like mien, the lowly "buzzard" spends its day cleaning up the grisly messes that others make. And we should be thankful that they do what they do.

The bird's scientific name, *Cathartes aura*, surprisingly means, "golden purifier," a hint that not all cultures disregard vultures as we most often do. So commonly seen along roadways that they go as unappreciated as garbage cans, turkey vultures have become fodder for "The Far Side" cartoons, wry puns, desert landscape art, and countless plots of Western novels.

It is a magnificent soaring bird, yet fate has cruelly bestowed upon it a whispy grunt or hiss rather than a majestic and searing screech. Its mute and patient circling suggests a grave robber rather than a powerful force of crucial cleaning efficiency; they are, putting it euphemistically, nature's custodial engineers.

It may be surprising, but buzzards—that name originated from the Latin for falcon, *buteo*—actually hang with impressive company. When looking for eagles or hawks, I usually first watch for the familiar gatherings of turkey vultures, for what they eat also ends up on the more respected raptors' tables as well. Two weeks ago, I captured a dramatic photo of a streaking young eagle that had been feeding on, shall I say, venison, with a band of buzzards. Without its yet-to-develop white head and tail feathers, he looked right at home on the ground with his less-appreciated pals.

Mike Lunsford

Living in the country, as we do, means that hardly a day passes without buzzards playing their silent, yet significant roles as stock characters. They glide above our woods and fields, often hanging above us as we work in the yard or head to the barn, not because—we hope—that they sense a prospective meal, but because they are curious birds that just happen to have terrific senses of both smell and sight. It is actually a myth that buzzards foretell death, a real comfort since a whole host of them whirled above my golfing buddies and me on a desperately hot day a few weeks ago.

It's said that buzzards can catch the scent of a meal from a mile away, yet, again, nature left them wanting; they have a pair of very puny legs, so weak that they cannot carry their rotting food with them. That is one reason they tend to remain with road kill impossibly long, often to their own misfortune.

Just a few years ago, a buzzard that just happened to choose the longest path between two points, smacked into and cracked the grill of my truck in its too-late attempt to get airborne; he survived the encounter. It is fact—and I hope you haven't just had breakfast—that buzzards, if threatened, will throw-up what they've last consumed just to lighten their load for take-off.

Of course, it is with death that buzzards are most often associated. Although a circling gang of vultures in flight is known as a "kettle" (the term may have come from the notion that the group resembles a boiling pot or cauldron), a passel of them feeding on a carcass is referred to as a "wake." I have to admit though that seeing a host of vultures ahead of me in the road or in a field reminds me more of buffet line than a funeral visitation.

It is a known fact that buzzards will also eat what other animals will not; to their credit, they can digest meat that may be in such an advanced state of decay that it can make other animals—particularly coyotes—sick. But because of their disgusting diets, buzzards clean our roadways and ditches, our pastures and waterways, which may very well be one of the most valuable services any animal provides.

This past spring, I wandered a local cemetery with my camera, looking for the bluebirds I had seen flitting from tombstone to tombstone a few weeks before. Instead, I spotted a turkey vulture as it perched on a rather shoddy nest of wild grapevines and dead branches that lay on the interior iron ladder rungs of an abandoned and roofless old concrete silo. There was no way to tell whether the bird was sitting on eggs, or even if it was a male or female. As is often the case in the bird world, the female is larger than the male. Yet, it sat, a quiet sentinel stoically watching to see how close I would come.

Despite their craven image as stealthy pursuers of decomposition, turkey vultures are highly sociable animals that spend time roosting in large colonies. Graceful in what appears to be an overstuffed winter coat, they often ride thermals like the most exalted of birds, their silver underfeathers often catching the sunlight. In what looks like a show of bravado, buzzards will spread their considerable wings, not as a show of force, but rather to allow their feathers to dry in the sun. Their bare and hideous red necks and faces—that look nearly sunburned—remain featherless to prevent bacteria from infecting them.

Until I began to research buzzards, I never knew that they actually have their own holiday, "International Vulture Awareness Day," which is celebrated on the first Saturday of each September.

I missed it this year, but I hope somebody had a banquet.

JIM AND CLARA'S BOYS
November 11, 2019

Although I was barely out of grade school before she died, I got to know my great-grandmother, Clara. She often stayed with my grandparents, living out of their spare room and her two suitcases before moving on to board at yet another son or daughter's place for a few months.

Clara's husband, James Lunsford, came home from his job as a county road worker one late winter afternoon in 1948, sat down on the couch and died; he was 70, but never knew retirement. Together, they had ten children and a large extended family, but none of them had yet tasted much prosperity—coal miners and WPA workers and farm hands, mostly—so he just kept trying to bring home a paycheck. After Jim died, Clara lived the rest of her life as a

This Old World

bit of a nomad, never staying anywhere long enough to have a real home again.

I mention that story on this Veterans Day, because until not long ago, when I spoke with a Colorado cousin who is studying our family's history, I never really thought much about the worry and tears Jim and Clara had invested in raising their family, in sending most of their boys off to war, in losing one of them who is buried in France. Together, they saw nine of their sons, sons-in-law, and grandsons wear a uniform in World War II: six serving in the European Theater, and three others headed to the Pacific.

Although I often spent time with Clara in my grandparents' too-warm and nearly silent house, she never spoke of her husband or her boys to me, at least as far as I remember. Born in 1884, she had already lived a long, tough life, and I mostly recall seeing her nestled in an armchair, darning socks, and silently grinning at my grandfather's silliness; he was among her oldest children, a bit too young for the Great War, a bit too old for World War II.

Clara once told me about seeing Buffalo Bill's Wild West Show when it came to Terre Haute, and about going to listen to William Howard Taft when he came to speak in Rockville for the Chautauqua in 1915. But mostly, I used to sit in the living room with her and peer through her ornate stereoscope, which eventually ended up in my grandmother's bedroom closet. It was hard to imagine then that she had ever been young, particularly as I observed her wrinkled eyes as they were magnified through her wiry gold eyeglasses; sometimes, the only sound in the house was the solitary tick of an ancient mantle clock.

Even then, I think I saw Clara's life as a sort of open history book, but one not turned to the pages about the war, nor including the photo of her long-gone husband, or one that mentioned the son who never came home, ever. She—nobody in the family, really—spoke of those things.

I have written before about Albert, one of her youngest boys. Good looking and popular, he was killed by a German fighter jet somewhere between Oberhoffen and Hagenau, France, in January 1945. In my mind, I see Jim and Clara at their kitchen table in the half-light of evening, staring at the cable informing them of Albert's death, whether that is the way it happened or not. However it went, the message arrived a day or so before the last of Albert's letters came to them in the mail. In it, he spoke of how good it had been to see his younger brother, Bob, just a day or two before; Bob even included a few lines in the letter himself.

Although I saw my Uncle Bob at family reunions and on fishing trips and knew he had been to war too, I didn't know that he was the first of his family to go to the service. He was a corporal in the Army, a chain-smoking lineman in a wire section who came home to be an electrician. He died at 59, and even though he never spoke of the war to me—as tight-lipped as his mother, I guess—I

This Old World

feel that he was, perhaps, the most affected by it; I'm not sure why.

Jim and Clara also watched as son, Charles William—we called him, Will—went off to Europe. He fought in the 85th Mountain Infantry, 10th Mountain Division, in Italy. Will was one of the most soft-spoken men I ever met, and my grandfather often took me up to the garage Will owned in Kingman. He was a mechanic, and I remember being most impressed with how he had converted a big Chrysler of his to LP gas. It never really registered with me then that my grandfather was 15 years older than Will.

A fourth brother went to war too. Tom, the youngest, left high school for the Navy; he became an aviation mechanic and, fortunately, saw no action. Tom lived well into his 90s, and until I did a little digging for this story, had no idea that his middle name, Wood, was Clara's maiden name, as if she had saved it for the last child.

Jim and Clara also watched son-in-law, Everett Allen, leave for military service. My great-uncle saw action in the Rhineland from June 1944 through the end of the war, something I wouldn't have considered probable when I went to his home in eastern Clay County to fish in Deer Creek with my grandfather. But now, I think I understand a little more why Everett sought a quiet life as a farmer, and I can see him still, sitting in his "front room," reading the newspaper, a smoldering pipe clamped in his teeth.

Four grandsons went to war, too. William Albert

"Bill" Sneddon was in the Army Air Corps, a flight engineer and top turret gunner in a B-24 "Liberator" over Italy; he survived 33 missions. His cousin, Lloyd Howard Allen, was a radio operator and gunner in a B-17 "Flying Fortress," and he flew terrifying nighttime missions over Germany in 1944 and 1945. He was two years younger than Bill, but they died in the same year.

I don't think I ever met another of Jim and Clara's grandsons, Robert "Gene" Allen. He was a navigator and radio operator on a torpedo bomber that flew off the decks of the aircraft carrier, Cowpens, in the Pacific Theater. He was two years older than his cousin, Kenneth Wayne Sneddon, who was a private in the 5th Cavalry Division, an Army mortar gunner, but the war was pretty well over by the time he got to the Pacific, and luckily so, for like Will, he was training for an invasion of the Japanese mainland. It is his son, Jeff, who helped me put this story in order.

I wrote earlier that I hadn't given much thought before about the fear and anxiety that my great-grandparents must have had with their loved ones being in that terrible war, about the tragic loss they suffered. But as time passes, perhaps I've learned a little more about the important things in life, and I understand their sleepless nights and prayers and worries.

Jim and Clara gave the country their most precious possession: their boys, as did so many millions of other parents. Their sacrifice is what Veterans Day is about, too.

This Old World

THE MAKING OF MINER BROWN
October 13, 2019

For three men whose paths mingled in the black dust and flickering lamp light of southern Parke County's coal mines, Mordecai Brown, Ike Durrett, and Mark Clayton, Jr. met with far different fates.

By the fall of 1916—long after they had gone in separate directions—age and a tired arm ended Brown's pitching career, one that eventually sent him to the Hall of Fame in Cooperstown as a Chicago Cubs legend. Clayton and Durrett, still young men, died that year, and, ironically, both had once been known as better players before anyone had much heard of "Three-Finger" Brown.

Of course, "Miner" Brown's story is well-known. Born near tiny Nyesville in 1876, he overcame two childhood accidents—one horrific and involving a corn thresher—that left his right hand grimly disfigured. His subsequent work as a "checker" in local coal mines (a job he first took at 14), and inspiration from a former minor leaguer—ironically nicknamed "Legs"—led him to believe he could become not only a player, but a pitcher for local semi-professional teams.

Brown's first significant playing time didn't come until he was already 21, the *Terre Haute Tribune* referring to him as a third baseman for the Nyesville Reds in 1897. By the next season, he had moved south to Coxville, blessed with a job that although paying less than miners' wages, kept him clear of the deadly work in the often-flooded and always-treacherous coal shafts.

As biographer Scott Brown—a descendent of the pitcher and founder of the Mordecai Brown Legacy Foundation—co-wrote with Cindy Thompson in *Three-Finger, The Mordecai Brown Story* (University of Nebraska Press, 2006), a checker's job was to take care of the day-to-day record keeping, collect union dues, and even terminate unproductive or troublesome workers.

"It was a good job, much preferable to the work the miners endured underground… Mine shafts were roughly carved three feet high — just large enough to support the width of a narrow-gauge track, on which miniature coal cars traveled. The miners themselves rode on their stomachs while en route to their destination deep within the earth. Lying on their sides, they hacked at the earthen walls, unable to stand in the cramped shafts to swing their picks freely. Surrounded by darkness pierced only by the small carbide lights shining from their caps, the miners labored in chilling conditions…"

Coal miners' lives, often short and sometimes violent, were commonly mixed with debt and alcohol and sickness, and the graveyards near coal mining towns like Coxville are filled with their bones and those of their hard-scrabble wives and sickly tubercular children.

It was that hellish scenario that Clayton and Durrett most certainly knew well, although in their younger days both may have played more baseball for the mine teams than actually picked coal for the mine owners. Semi-professional baseball was a popular draw for area fans in those days when it took both sparse extra time and spare money to travel from the farm or coal fields to watch games in bigger venues such as Terre Haute. Rockville, Clinton, Shelburn, Rosedale, Brazil—even Catlin and Carbon—boasted competitive teams, and local merchants (the most prosperous at the time being mine owners) paid better wages to good talent. In some instances, they simply employed roaming players (particularly, pitchers) on a per-game basis; it's likely that Durrett and Clayton supplemented their incomes in such a way.

Isaac Durrett, born in Albermarle County, Virginia, in 1872, four years before Brown and Clayton, had a long playing career that included a dizzying list of stops over western Indiana and eastern Illinois, Michigan, Ohio, and points south. Described as "big and brawny," he was known to have pitched and played in the outfield for Dana, and Washington, Indiana, and in Danville and Oakland, Illinois. He was touted as playing for a "crack" team in Rockville in 1895, and would eventually play just below the Majors in the Western League in places such as Indianapolis, Grand Rapids, Springfield, and Toledo. By 1901, he was playing for the Chattanooga Lookouts with Clayton, and by 1904 was with the Montgomery, Alabama, Senators. In 1906, Durrett assaulted the manager of the rival Birmingham team while serving as the Senators skipper; after forfeiting the game, he was released. In box scores he shows up primarily as a leftfielder, although more than once he was described as a "hot" pitcher.

Durrett made Parke County headlines in December 1897 after being shot at a "bowl-up" Christmas celebration at the National Guard Armory. Although initial accounts said he was not expected to live, another depicted him as quickly recovering from a near-fatal wound. The incident would be far from the last brush with the law he would have.

Mark Clayton, Jr., was the son of a coal-mining father who emigrated from England to Parke County. Like Brown, he was born in 1876 and also aspired to get out of the mines and onto the diamond, which he did, pitching for a variety of teams, but most noticeably, Coxville by 1897. There were as many as 20 coal mines in the area between that town and Rosedale to the south, and manager Johnny Buckley had a considerable number of players from which to choose.

Clayton was noted as being "perhaps the best pitcher in the state," in one newspaper account, and "...was thought at the time as being better than Mordecai Brown" in another story published a few years later. Just three years after playing with Brown in Parke County, Clayton signed a contract to pitch for Chattanooga at $80 a month, good wages in those days. It was the first of four professional teams for which he would play. He spent a year with the Terre Haute Hottentots in 1902 (the year after Brown left the club), played with the Vincennes Reds in 1904, and was last known to have pitched for the Waterloo Microbes in

This Old World

1905.

Surely, 1898 was nearly as important a year for all three men as any in their lives. By Brown's own account, he was slated to play third base for Coxville (also named the Reds) in a highly-anticipated game with Brazil (big wagers were made on such games) at the Clay County Fairgrounds on July 22.

"When the game was called, Clayton appeared on the diamond, clad in his uniform, ready to play, but pickled to the gills…" Brown recalled. "The manager, John Buckley, saw his condition and ordered him not to play. He asked me to fill the box. I did, pitched seven innings without a man getting to first base, and we won 7-3." There is no reason not to believe—although I could find no box score of the game—that talented, but troublesome, Ike Durrett was also in uniform that day.

Although Brown stayed with Coxville after the Brazil game, and continued to pitch a little, it took long hours of practice before he developed what Ty Cobb would eventually call "the most devastating pitch" he ever faced: a sinking, fading, almost knuckleball-like curve. By the spring of 1899, he began stair-stepping his way to the National League, stopping for the 1901 season in Terre Haute's Three-I-League. Ironically, he was slated to be cut from the Hottentots, but his popularity led to a boycott and petition, so a man named Curtis was released instead.

Clayton and Durrett continued to hop from team to team, as well, but they never got their "cup of coffee" in the "bigs." Clayton's father died after falling into a coal car in 1900 (Clayton, Sr., and his wife are buried in Rockville), and little is known about his life after he left Parke County in 1901, except that he eventually stopped playing baseball and went back to mining coal, for the last time in Gibson County. He did serve a little time in jail for not financially supporting his family there.

Durrett's baseball career stalled out sometime after 1908, but he turned to other interests. Operating out of Terre Haute, Sullivan, Farmersburg, and Robinson, Illinois, he was involved in countless brawls, served time in jail for robbery, was tried for larceny, was accused of running several "blind tigers" (illegal bars), got involved in a prostitution operation, and tried his hand in local politics. It purportedly took over "a hundred stitches" to close the wounds he received in a knife fight in Terre Haute.

On February 19, 1916, a farmer came across Durrett's body near Graysville in Sullivan County. Referred to in newspaper accounts as a "riverman from Old York," Illinois, Durrett was found shoeless in the mud and ice of a flooded cornfield; it was determined that a few days before he had managed to cross the currents of the full and partially-frozen Wabash River in a row boat, only to come ashore in the dark, become disoriented in the cold, and drown in a pond.

In perhaps the most ironic twist to his story, the Sullivan County sheriff, Ed Kelly—to whom Ike Durrett was no stranger—described for the local papers the day he watched Mordecai Brown pitch his first real game in Brazil in 1898; Kelly claimed it was Durrett, not Clayton, that Brown replaced on the mound that day.

Clayton moved to Oakland City, Indiana, sometime after 1905. He married a widow there and found work digging coal in the Muren Mine. There, on Saturday morning, July 8, 1916, a month shy of his 40th birthday, he was killed by falling slate. His death certificate reads that Clayton's body was taken to Rosedale for burial, but in one final slight to the man who was once "better than Mordecai Brown," there is no record of his being buried anywhere in Parke County.

THE FLEXIBLE FLYER OF MEMORY
December 16, 2019

Years ago, in the days when school snow days were considered "acts of God" and arrived silently unburdened with the weight of e-learning and extended academic calendars, I spent those precious and rare winter breaks on the hill across the road from our house with few cares in the world, sledding.

Play is the universal language of children—even old ones like me—and so, despite a trend toward plastic rather than wood and steel, sledding remains a popular pastime that will never be dated or forgotten.

If experienced properly, a snow day spent outdoors with companions provides the best science, civics, and physical education classes there are, so it also behooves adults to do something about removing the nagging thoughts all school kids must suffer about having extra days tacked onto the end of their school year...

I live on a rolling and uneven place now, but, ironically, we don't have one decent sledding hill. That was not the case when I was a boy; my aunt and uncle's property across the County Line Road was dominated by a huge hill—a real death-defying, luge-ready, break-neck grade, topped by a massive beech tree that blocked the north wind between our runs down a south-facing slope toward a ditch that was more than broad enough to keep us from hurtling into the road.

When I think of the hours I spent playing there with my brother and sister and cousins, I wonder just how I never had frostbite nor suffered a broken bone. Come to think of it though, I believe I'd still give at least one frozen pinky toe to be sledding there again. In those days, sleds, of course, came equipped primarily with a pair of metal runners; we associated classic toboggans with old movies and toy catalogues and New England. Although we had a decrepit sled of our own, and still used it when necessary, we normally enjoyed the superiority of our cousins' sleds— one of which my Aunt Eleanor won in a drawing at Wilbur Hickman's IGA in Rosedale.

By the time we pulled the sleds off the garage walls for the season—usually prayers for snow began just after Halloween and carried through March—their runners were rusty brown and dull. Before ever bothering with my uncle's bench grinder, we usually tried to scour the corrosion off with a rock; waxed paper was then promptly used on the runners between "coasts."

In fact, any substance that could improve the tribology (yes, I looked that term up; it means, "the science and engineering of interacting surfaces in relative motion") of our fun was worth a shot. If I recall correctly, I may have even run my dripping nose across the runners in an attempt to improve both speed and distance; Crisco was often a consideration too.

We were a ragtag outfit and mostly wore a grubby array of old blue jeans and sweatshirts, stocking caps and wool mittens, and, of course, did so over a layer of nubby long cotton underwear, a scratchy muffler often wrapped around our heads. Sodden and half-frozen, we'd take a break at lunch, sometimes basking in the glorious heat of my grandparents' coal-fired kitchen or draping our clothes across a utility room register. A bowl of soup and a change of clothes later, we'd be chugging our way up the hill again, pulling our sleds by the ropes we looped through the pre-drilled holes in the cross-arms.

Although it was most often my sister, Lora, and my cousin, Renee, and I out both first and the longest, we were sometimes joined by our older brothers, who not only displayed more guts, but also scientific reasoning to our sledding technology. Both about six years older than me, my cousin, Roger, and brother John,—who eventually built a dangerous snowmobile out of a sled and an ancient rotary mower — loved to fire up my uncle's Ford 8N tractor, chain the rusted hood of a late 40s Plymouth to the hitch, have us pile onto old chair cushions, then take us off down the road a few miles for a bumpy ride to Joppa.

It's at this point that I probably should provide the disclaimer: DO NOT TRY THIS AT HOME. Inevitably, Roger would pin one of the tractor's brakes and get the hood flinging at near-centrifugal force, and it never really occurred to any of us that we should be scared. My aunt once told Renee that she watched us through a kitchen window as we skidded across a flower bed embankment and bucked—it is important here that you know we were being supervised by an adult—into the air. "All I could see were flying arms and legs," she said.

If memory serves me right, only one of our sleds was an original "Flexible Flyer," the brand to which all others were compared. Flyers were patented by Samuel Leeds Allen in 1889, and one report suggests that he—like my brother and cousin—used "local children and adults to test prototypes."

Using the Flyer's pivoting handles enabled the operator to steer, not only by hand, but with the feet. It goes without saying that we rode our sleds lying prone on our bellies, sitting upright, even blindly backwards, and since only one of the sleds was long enough for us to stretch out completely, we had to ride the shorter ones with our feet dangling and dripping above our backs. Truly, our bellowing screams of delight still ring in my head, and if I imagine it long enough, I can yet feel the sting of frozen slush hitting my face and the tiredness of my legs by the time I had reached the summit of the hill to do it all over again.

Renee tells me that one of the old sleds still hangs in her garage, and I hope one of her many grandkids drags it out and scrapes off its years of rust with a rock. The hill and the homeplace were sold years ago; the beech, dying bit by bit, dropped its rope swing and finally fell in a storm.

But, in the flexible flyer of memory, I am again nine years old, and red-faced, very cold, and happy.

THE REAL VALUE OF FIELD TRIPS
December 30, 2019

Although he is best remembered for his "experiment in living" near Walden Pond, Henry David Thoreau was, among other things, a teacher. Not long after resigning from Concord's Center School, whose administrator had ordered him to use corporal punishment to keep his students under control, the Harvard-educated Thoreau found himself teaching again, this time with his brother, John, his best friend. It was 1839.

The Thoreaus taught together two years, but eventually quit the profession when John's tuberculosis worsened. By all accounts they were innovative and popular teachers who regularly took their students out of the classroom, granted them much longer recesses, and in one instance, even had their charges help with tarring the bottom of their rowboat, a very practical skill to have in those days.

Henry and John believed in what I grew up calling, "field trips," although, it is important to add that they often instructed their students with very traditional methods and in classical subjects; it seems that rote learning and memorization had places in their curriculum, too.

But the brothers also opened their classroom's windows for the fresh air, a practice that was hardly conventional in the days when teachers ruled with stern authority and expected the undivided attention of their students.

They also regularly took long walks in the fields and woods around the busy Massachusetts town—just north and west of Boston—yet, advocating that their students learn trades, they conducted tours of local businesses, including the print and gun shops.

Henry wrote in his journal, "We should seek to be fellow students with the pupil, and we should learn of, as well as with him, if we would be most helpful to him." With that concept very much in play, Thoreau mastered the fundamentals of surveying while he and his students took a field trip to analyze the height and size of Fair Haven Hill. This teacher of Greek and French and Physics truly advocated "life-long" learning, for he became everything from carpenter to pencil maker to stonemason to poet, and he eventually supported himself off-and-on as a surveyor.

Despite my growing intolerance of the cold weather

that plagued us in late fall, I have been taking my own field trips—now, often called "study trips"—into the countryside, and I have seen plenty: eagles and hawks; the abstract designs of frozen pond ice; the work of beavers; the early-evening hunting of short-eared owls; the tracks of bobcats and coyotes.

As a teacher, I decided long ago that it was almost always a good thing to get my students out of their chairs, to stir their blood, to get them moving, for the habit led them to think and question; it seems to work that way for me, as well.

There is something about walking in the woods, sometimes with my grandson or daughter or wife—but most often alone—that helps me make some sense of the noise I hear on the news, through social media, through nuisance calls and sales pitches. Nature, it seems, forces me to bear down a bit and listen and observe and ponder.

A few weeks ago, the day after a few inches of snowfall, and with the promise of more to come that night, my oldest grandson, who is four, came over for the day. He expected me to take him for a walk; I had expected him to ask. Although it was in the low 20s, the sun was covered by clouds, and a brisk north breeze blew in our faces as we headed out the door. Knowing that he had recently outgrown his boots, his mother had packed an old pair of hers for him in the hope he could play a while outdoors while she shopped that very day for new ones. The boots were clownishly big, but he assured us that they were fine, and so we left.

Because it was slick and mostly downhill, he walked in my shadow and in my footsteps. Because the boots were awkward, we plodded, which suited him well, for it seemed as though he had something to say about nearly everything he saw. We heard the jays and woodpeckers squawking high above us, and he asked more than once about another bird he was hearing—a little nuthatch that we eventually spotted just as he scrabbled head-first down a fat wild grape vine.

With a half-hour or so behind us, he pronounced us "lost," that his grandmother would be missing us, but it was his cold face and wet hands that convinced me that we needed to end the field trip in favor of something warm to drink, and that by the time we walked back—uphill much of the way—it would be enough for the day.

As we headed home, following his suggestion that we walk in the footprints we had left coming down, his borrowed boots, now thoroughly soaked, began to slip off his feet. With the worst of the climb yet to go, I knew I would have to eventually carry him on my back the rest of the way, or his grandmother might, indeed, be sending out a hunting party; it proved to be a tough climb.

Perhaps on that day, I reaffirmed two things: that my physical conditioning has slipped, and that these "adventure" days have helped me get to know my grandson better. Together, we have traveled to the creek to walk sandbars and to the woods to learn the trees, but I have also taken him along to the recycling center and the hardware store, to the county courthouse and to lunch with my old buddies. He is discovering, despite already being a decided homebody, that there is a world, and we must learn to live in it.

In another journal entry, still timely, although written 160 years ago, Thoreau says that it would be worthwhile to introduce children to a grove of primitive oaks before the trees "...are all gone, instead of hiring botanists to lecture to them when it is too late."

OLD SOLDIERS NEVER DIE
January 13, 2020

Joanie and I are the children of the children of the Great Depression. Our parents and their parents grew up saving things, storing things, stacking up and packing away things, because they just might be needed or wanted, by somebody, someday...

Surely, we all had a grandma who couldn't bear to throw an old calendar or catalog away, a mother who wiped down and re-used aluminum foil, a grandfather or dad who kept "doodads" and "thingamabobs" in old coffee cans and halved milk jugs. We grew up with "junk drawers" and full closets and cardboard boxes under our beds. We had no garage when I was a boy, but if we had, it would have been full.

Because of these nearly genetic predispositions, Joanie and I have saved and stored and packed too, but we are at a point where we now realize that we have far too much, and some of it has to go somewhere else before it simply becomes a burden to our children. It is going to be a long and difficult thinning process.

Of course, much of what we have tucked away—most likely sealed in totes and taped in boxes and twist-tied into garbage bags—already belongs to our kids, adults now with houses and lives, and hopefully, bare storage sheds and empty closets of their own.

Resistant in the past to taking on much of the accumulation themselves, we saw a vital crack in their defenses when my son innocently suggested that as we pulled our Christmas decorations out this winter, that perhaps we could look for his old Lego sets so his two boys could have them.

He should have kept his mouth shut.

As we do each first weekend of December, we began the arduous and tiring task of digging out Christmas lights and wrapping paper and gift boxes, my wife's snowman collection, wreaths, garlands and sleds, and the three artificial trees I put up in the yard. We have too many decorations, most unused now, and Joanie said with grim determination that what wasn't being put out or lit up this year wasn't going back into the storage barn.

So, with her playing the role of Hiram Bigham at Machu Pichu, I opened our storage shed attic and stood by as she braved a few cobwebs and dark corners and unearthed a cardboard box labeled: "Lego Sets." But she

This Old World

was far from finished; nearby, she saw a few totes with our daughter's name on them, a box or two titled, "Remote-Controlled Cars," and another, boldly tagged, "Army Men."

With more yet to explore, but our decorations strewn on the field of battle and in need of attention, we set aside four containers for our daughter, and quite a few more for our son. I immediately loaded the latter into my truck and delivered them to him within the half-hour. Wisely, I handed him the box of Legos first; then, while he was preoccupied, I quietly dropped my tail gate...

I kept the soldiers. Most were mine anyway, left over from childhood days when virtually every toy I owned was stowed under my bed in a single cardboard box. I had given them to my son years ago, but in a moment of nostalgia I told Joanie I wanted to sort through the boxes and look for the oldest, those in service now well over a half-century, battle-tested, scarred from a thousand summer afternoons, battered and broken and dirty and unforgettable.

I spent part of an evening sorting through the box, and although many of my favorite soldiers had been scattered to the wind or buried in the trenches of our back yard years ago, some had survived their boxed and silent bivouac in storage. Among them, a few hand-painted cavalry men who fought near my plastic Fort Apache stockade, a few more from a Civil War set, forever dressed in blue and gray, and still more, inspired by the hours I spent in front of our television watching *Combat*. The troops included a pair of grimy GIs that looked remarkably like Ric Jason and Vic Morrow; I even had a few Nazis left. I told Joanie that I just couldn't let them go, and she promptly labeled a new box, "Mike's Toys."

Our grandsons visit us a few days a week; just long enough to deplete our snacks and ransack our house. While the older spends his mornings in pre-school, the younger occupies his time playing with trains, begging for oatmeal, and chattering like a woodpecker. A few days ago, I walked into our spare bedroom to see him and his grandmother sitting on the floor, reading a book amid a pile of wooden blocks and wrecked tractors.

As I grabbed his bare ankles, he reacted to my cold hands. "He needs long socks," I told Joanie. "Maybe we should buy him some, long winter ones, when we go into town today."

She nodded, but a light bulb popped on in her head and she said, "Wait, I have some already. I think they're in the back closet; I bought them years ago."

Well, we can't just get rid of everything…

This Old World

Also by MIKE LUNSFORD

The Off Season: The Newspaper Stories of Mike Lunsford
ISBN: 978-0-615-23811-1

Sidelines: the Best of the Basketball Stories
ISBN: 978-0-615-30731-2

A Place Near Home
ISBN 978-0-615-49749-5

A Windy Hill Almanac
ISBN: 978-0-615-76553-2

The Bridge That Carries You Over
ISBN: 978-0-692-46301-7

Field Notes and Other Stories...
ISBN: 978-0-692-91115-0

Mike Lunsford

This Old World